Penguin Books

australian
gardening
calendar

australian gardening calendar

Penguin Books

PENGUIN BOOKS

UK | USA | Canada | Ireland | Australia
India | New Zealand | South Africa | China

Penguin Books is part of the Penguin Random House group of companies
whose addresses can be found at global.penguinrandomhouse.com.

Penguin
Random House
Australia

First published by Penguin Books Australia Ltd, 1993
This revised edition published by Penguin Group (Australia), 2005

Cover design by Louise Leffler © Penguin Group (Australia)
Text design by Louise Leffler and Elizabeth Dias © Penguin Group (Australia)
Cover photograph by Francesca Yorke/Getty Images
Typeset in Frutiger Light 9.75/15.75 pt by Post Pre-press Group, Brisbane, Queensland
Printed and bound in Australia by Griffin Press, an accredited
ISO AS/NZS 14001 Environmental Management Systems printer.

A catalogue record for this
book is available from the
National Library of Australia

NATIONAL
LIBRARY
OF AUSTRALIA

ISBN 978 0 14 300246 8

MIX
Paper | Supporting
responsible forestry
FSC® C018684

penguin.com.au

contents

introduction

When do I plant daffodil bulbs? What's the best month for pruning roses? Will my Iceland poppies be blooming in September? Some of the most common questions asked by home gardeners relate to timing, and the *Australian Gardening Calendar* sets out to answer them.

No one should be too dismayed at finding the clock has beaten them, however. Experienced gardeners know that they can sometimes get excellent results outside the most favourable times. And the location of your garden – by the sea, far inland, or on a wind-swept hill – may shift the dates some weeks in either direction. Personal circumstances often come into it too. If you take your holidays in July every year, and go away for the whole month, you will never be able to prune your roses at exactly the recommended time. But late June or early August will be very nearly as good anyway.

The greatest variations in the gardening year arise from the climatic differences between the cool to temperate parts of Australia and the subtropical to tropical regions. Each chapter is therefore divided into two sections so that these distinct zones receive individual attention. They are very broad zones, of course. The areas designated cool–temperate encompass the south-west corner of Western Australia, Adelaide and environs, southern Victoria, southern New South Wales and Tasmania. And there is no clearcut boundary between the zones. Those who travel up the east coast, shedding layers of clothing as they go, will have experienced gradual changes in temperature, crops and natural vegetation that signify their approach to the subtropical and tropical north.

Gardeners need to know *how* as well as *when* to take cuttings, plant their trees, and divide perennials. They also want sensible suggestions on what to plant where. You'll find all this in the following pages.

january

a month for taking stock

JOB FILE

- *Mulch the garden thoroughly*
- *Harvest vegetables while they are young*
- *Protect fruit from birds*
- *Take softwood and semi-hardwood cuttings to grow new plants*
- *Watch out for fungal diseases*
- *Cut lawns, but no shorter than 2 cm*
- *Water plants deeply: don't just spray the surface*
- *Deadhead and fertilise roses*
- *Ask a friend to garden-sit if you go away*

Throughout Australia, January is a good month for taking stock of your garden.

- Does it please or disappoint you?
- Can you cope with its demands?
- Is there enough shade?

a pleasing garden

Few people who find their gardens pleasing are complacent about them for long. Some plants pass their peak in a few days, and weeds can spring up overnight. There is always something to improve on, a corner to renovate, some new combination to try.

But a garden that is never more than mediocre needs attention. If one of your New Year resolutions is to make an unsatisfactory garden more attractive, this may be an excellent time for starting – particularly if there is a cool spell between hot days. It is much easier to analyse a garden's faults when it has had a good clean-up.

- Mow lawn and rough grass, catching or raking clippings for mulch.
- Dig out spring annuals that have finished flowering (save some seed – Shirley poppies, love-in-the-mist – for autumn sowing in cool and temperate gardens).
- Deadhead untidy perennials and shrubs.
- Loosen soil with a fork and pull out noticeable weeds.
- Water bare soil deeply and cover with mulch 15 cm thick.

Then check the garden for:

- impact (more colour or better colour combinations?)
- balance (more shrubs or fewer annuals?)
- interesting elements (mounds, steps or seats?).

If the weather is hot, some quiet planning, stimulated by garden magazines and cool drinks, may be your most important step towards a more pleasing garden in the months to come.

a manageable garden

Your garden may be too big or too complex to deal with comfortably. Here are some suggestions for simplifying it.

- Reduce areas of lawn, which consume excessive amounts of water.
- Plant low shrubs and scramblers to cover bare ground and suppress weeds.
- Concentrate on caring for the plants that are most valuable to you, and don't worry about the rest.
- Install automatic watering systems. Find out about the laws governing their use in your area.
- Invest in a little paid help if possible.

a shady garden

Summer is the time to test a garden for shadiness, but it is important to allow plenty of light to penetrate at cooler and cloudier times of the year too.

Trees that are bare in winter but give deep shade in summer are very useful for sun control, and so are pergolas that can be fitted with shadecloth in summer and opened up in winter (deciduous creepers will have the same effect). In the southern states, light-foliaged evergreens like *Eucalyptus nicholii* and *E. pulchella* offer a compromise between deciduous trees and dense evergreens like the various cypresses. The poinciana (*Delonix regia*) is a popular deciduous tree for subtropical and tropical regions, where it has a similar role to the deciduous oaks, elms and ashes in offering shade variation for the different seasons.

cool & temperate zones

Spring annuals have gone to seed, many roses are taking a break, and the bright bottlebrush flowers of *Callistemon* species have degenerated into rusty-looking seedheads – unless you did the right thing and pruned them straight after they flowered.

January gardens in southern Australia can be a little drab unless they are carefully planned. If your garden failed the impact test you will have to wait until at least autumn for a major replanting program focused on colour, though any flower seedlings available (such as those in the January list) will be looking good quite soon.

Trees for improved shadiness are also best planted in autumn or winter for gardens in temperate areas, in spring in the coldest regions.

COOL & TEMPERATE ZONES

flowers to plant

Seed

ageratum
forget-me-not
gypsophila*
Iceland poppy*
larkspur*
linaria*
lupin
mignonette*
pansy
portulaca
stock

Seedlings

delphinium
dianthus

vegetables to plant

Seed

beetroot*
broccoli
cabbage
cauliflower
celery
lettuce*
parsnip*
radish*
silver beet

Seedlings

broccoli
cauliflower
celery
leek
silver beet

*Seed of these plants is best sown straight into the garden. Others should be sown in containers for transplanting later, or may be available now as seedlings.

other jobs for january

- Water garden as permitted by the laws of your area.
- Deadhead roses. Fertilise with cow manure and potash, or a special rose mixture. Spray with triflorine if black spot is evident.
- Apply liquid fertiliser to fuchsias and cut back those that have finished flowering.
- Keep annual and perennial flowers blooming by sprinkling with liquid fertiliser fortnightly.
- Dig potatoes and harvest onions when they are mature.
- Weed and fertilise vegetables, and pick crops regularly.
- Take softwood and semi-hardwood cuttings to grow new plants.
- Remove excessive runners from strawberry plants.
- Re-pot cyclamen.
- Spray apple and pear trees with carbaryl every three weeks to protect against codling and light brown apple moth.

looking good down south

- Sweetcorn nearly ready to pick, on plants 1.5 m tall; zucchini – finger-size to outsize in a week
- The native shrub crowea, covered with waxy deep pink flowers; the exotic abelia, with arching wands of pale pink bells

COOL & TEMPERATE ZONES

- The large yellow blooms of the twining guinea flower (*Hibbertia scandens*)
- The South African daphne (*Dais cotinifolia*), a small tree with 5 cm pink pompoms; the Australian leatherwood (*Eucryphia lucida*), with large white or pale-pink flowers

watering

Though we must be careful not to waste a scarce resource, and to abide by the usage laws that exist in each state, it is necessary in many Australian gardens to water artificially in summer. Most well-established trees and shrubs need little extra moisture, but new and shallow-rooted plants will not survive without help. Make judicious use of watering aids:

- timers – invaluable whether taps are operated manually or automatically
- drippers – very economical in their use of water, but unpleasant-looking when piping is above ground and prone to clogging when it is buried
- sprinklers – more wasteful than drippers because of evaporation, but almost maintenance-free.

subtropical & tropical zones

Gardens in the settled areas of the north rarely lack colour, but some of them could do with more shade even in winter. Be sure to check shade levels when stocktaking, and plan some long-term improvements if necessary. Three large, shady trees for planting in mild weather are described at the end of this chapter.

flowers to plant

Seed or seedlings

ageratum

amaranthus*

celosia

coleus

salvia

sunflower

torenia

vegetables to plant

Seed or seedlings

capsicum

cauliflower

celery

eggplant

lettuce*

silver beet

sweetcorn*

*Seed of these plants is best sown straight into the garden. Others should be sown in containers for transplanting later, or may be available now as seedlings.

other jobs for january

- Check that the garden is as secure as possible against wild winds and sudden downpours.
- Water as permitted (in the morning preferably, to reduce the incidence of fungal diseases).
- Renew mulches as they decompose.
- Keep annual and perennial flowers blooming by sprinkling with liquid fertiliser fortnightly.
- Prune bougainvilleas as they finish flowering.
- Hang fruit fly baits in fruit trees and collect fallen fruit (destroy any that is infected).
- Check pots and hanging baskets daily but do not over-water them.
- Weed vegetables well and fertilise them, picking crops frequently. Vegetables usually need more water than most other plants.
- Take softwood and semi-hardwood cuttings to grow new plants.
- Plant sweet potatoes in the vegetable garden.
- Lay snailbait after rain.

looking good up north

- Agapanthus (blue, white) and cannas (red, orange)
- The little blue butterfly bush (*Clerodendrum ugandense*) has sprays of blue flowers

- The lady slipper vine (*Thunbergia mysorensis*), with brown and orange flowers
- The small tree known as golden shower (*Cassia fistula*) has clusters of yellow flowers
- Two large native trees: yellow poinciana (*Peltophorum pterocarpum*), with sprays of yellow flowers at the top; Illawarra flame tree (*Brachychiton acerifolius*), with red flowers on leafless branches

shade for northern gardens

Here are three intensely shady trees for tempering the heat and humidity in large subtropical and tropical gardens.

- *Harpullia pendula* (tulipwood)

  A very attractive native (to 15 m tall) with a spreading crown. Sprays of yellowish summer flowers are followed by orange capsules.
- *Mangifera indica* (mango)

  Although fruit bats may make a mess when the fruit ripens in summer, mangoes are excellent trees for shade. Seedlings can grow to 40 m, but grafted trees are smaller and produce better fruit.
- *Pithecellobium saman* (rain tree, far north only)

  The shady leaflets of this tree (to 24 m tall) fold together during rain. The pretty summer flowers are deep pink.

SUBTROPICAL & TROPICAL ZONES

february

a month for sowing seed

JOB FILE

- *Keep up the watering as permitted by the laws of your area*
- *Remove summer annuals as they finish flowering*
- *Order spring-flowering bulbs*
- *Check the garden after summer downpours: is there too much runoff or flooding?*
- *Trim summer-flowering shrubs as they fade*
- *Watch out for fungal diseases*
- *Take softwood and semi-hardwood cuttings to grow new plants*
- *Erect shadecloth screens for tender plants*

This is not the only month suitable for sowing the seed of flowers and vegetables in containers, but the weather generally favours germination and most of the resulting seedlings should be big enough to plant out in autumn. This means that they will flower or produce crops by late winter or spring in cool and temperate areas, earlier in warmer regions.

Some flowers and vegetables do better if sown straight into finely raked soil in garden beds (see the asterisks in the sowing lists each month). Sowing in containers and then transplanting the seedlings is a little more complicated. Raising your own plants by either of these methods has several advantages.

- A packet holding a number of seeds, usable for two or three years, is usually much cheaper than a punnet of seedlings.
- You can grow varieties rarely stocked by nurseries but obtainable from specialist firms and organisations.
- There will be gifts of seedlings for friends and relatives if all goes well.

equipment

Anyone can get seed to germinate without sophisticated or expensive equipment. Here are the basics:

- sterilised containers with drainage holes (shallow trays or boxes, pierced ice-cream containers, or pots, preferably plastic, that are wide at the top)
- a suitable medium – a sterilised commercial mix (available from a nursery or supermarket), or about three parts of coarse sand to one part of peat moss or sieved compost
- a trigger-controlled sprayer for the hose
- a position that is warm (but not hot), sheltered (but not cold) and conveniently located.

procedure

Prepare containers by washing them, then soaking for ten minutes in household bleach diluted one part to twenty parts of water. Home-made mixes of sand and peat will be less likely to transmit disease to plants if boiling water is poured over them near sowing time. The next steps are as follows:

- Sow the seed thinly in the damp mix. This will be easy if each seed is big enough to handle, more difficult if it is tiny. Mixing very fine seed with dry sand will improve its dispersal.
- Plant large seeds at a depth similar to their diameter, and barely cover fine seed.
- Label each container with plant name and date of sowing (a waterproof marker in a contrasting colour is best).
- Water very lightly once the seed is sown; placing the container in a tray of water will help keep it damp. A fungicide watered in soon after planting time will reduce the risk of fungal disease.

Keep up the gentle watering until you have strong 5 cm seedlings ready for transferring into small individual pots. These too should be sterilised before being filled with commercial or home-made potting mix. Press each little plant firmly into place and water well, consolidating the soil around it. Half-strength liquid fertiliser will give the plants a boost after the first week.

Provided that you do not let the seedlings dry out, they should be ready to move into the garden in autumn. Dig some compost into the soil and sprinkle a pinch of complete fertiliser around each plant. Once again you will have to water the seedlings straight away, but thereafter only during dry spells. Protect your plants with snailbait, but ask for a variety that is not harmful to pets.

Use liquid fertiliser fortnightly, and apply derris dust to any seedlings that belong to the cabbage family.

cool & temperate zones

In Tasmania and southern Victoria you may need to place containers where they receive direct sunshine for part of the day, though keeping them moist will be especially important in such positions. Early germination will ensure that seedlings are growing strongly before the weather cools.

Around Perth and Adelaide, and north of the ranges in Victoria, sowing for spring flowers and vegetables can continue through March and April, and the transplanting of seedlings into June.

flowers to plant

Seed

alyssum
calendula
candytuft
Canterbury bell
cineraria
columbine
cornflower*
delphinium
English daisy*
forget-me-not
gaillardia
gypsophila*
Iceland poppy*
larkspur*
linaria*
lobelia*

love-in-the-mist*
lupin
mignonette*
nasturtium*
pansy
petunia
stock
sweet pea*
Virginian stock*
wallflower

Seedlings

alyssum
delphinium
dianthus

vegetables to plant

Seed	*Seedlings*
beetroot*	broccoli
broccoli	cabbage
cabbage	celery
cauliflower	leek
lettuce*	silver beet
leek	
onion, white*	
parsnip*	
radish*	
silver beet	
spinach	

*Seed of these plants is best sown straight into the garden. Others should be sown in containers for transplanting later, or may be available now as seedlings.

first aid for house-plants

Are your hanging baskets, pot-plants and tub-plants in good health?
If not, give them a pick-me-up now.

- Trim off dead flowers, yellowing leaves and dry stems.
- Dunk very dry containers in a bucket or trough of water until bubbling stops.

COOL & TEMPERATE ZONES

- Move plants to shadier or less draughty spots if they are drying out too quickly.
- Mist-spray fine leaves, and wipe larger, shiny leaves with a cloth dipped in diluted white oil (to reduce scale and mealybug attack).
- Add shadecloth to pergolas and patios if direct sun is penetrating.
- Put plants outside in gentle rain for an hour or so.
- If a plant still looks poor after a week, chop it into the compost and buy another.

other jobs for february

- Plan autumn bulb-planting.
- Water garden as permitted.
- Keep annual and perennial flowers blooming by sprinkling with liquid fertiliser fortnightly.
- Weed and fertilise vegetables, and pick crops regularly.
- Take softwood cuttings of shrubs (see 'Taking cuttings' on page 26).
- Prune geraniums and pot up 15 cm cuttings from the prunings.
- Check roses for powdery mildew and black spot (spray with triforine if necessary).
- Spray apple and pear trees with carbaryl every three weeks to protect against codling and light brown apple moth.
- Prune buddlejas heavily when they have finished flowering.

- Prune large hydrangeas to half-size when they have finished flowering.
- Check lawns for the fungal disease dollar spot (look for the characteristic cobwebby brown patches) and spray with triadimefon or benomyl if necessary.
- Prepare ground for autumn seedlings where summer annuals have been cleared.
- Late in the month plant nerine bulbs; include some white ones for Mother's Day.

looking good down south

- Belladonnas ranging from white to pink; orange–red Scarborough lilies
- Cosmos and petunias, flowering endlessly
- Hybrid roses, undamaged by aphis or thrip
- Moonah (*Melaleuca lanceolata*), 6 m tall and crowded with neat white bottlebrush flowers

COOL & TEMPERATE ZONES

subtropical & tropical zones

In the humidity of a northern summer, seeds of flowers and vegetables germinate quickly and cuttings take root readily. Plant diseases, however, also flourish under these conditions.

Be meticulous in your sterilising of propagation equipment, and allow plenty of airflow around containers.

'Damping-off' is a rotting disease usually caused by fungi and capable of destroying whole pots of newly planted seeds, seedlings and cuttings. Watering the soil in containers with a fungicide will help to prevent damping-off and can also rescue mildly affected plants. Ask your supplier for one that contains furalaxyl, and follow the directions on the pack.

Though pots need an airy spot, shade from the sun and protection from rain are just as important. The cyclone season makes the sowing of seed and the planting of seedlings in the open garden more of a gamble than usual.

flowers to plant

Seed

ageratum

celosia

coleus

Iceland poppy*

lobelia*

salvia

sunflower

Seedlings

ageratum

celosia

coleus

salvia

sunflower

torenia

zinnia

vegetables to plant

Seed

beetroot*

capsicum

carrot*

cauliflower

celery

cucumber*

eggplant

lettuce*

marrow*

Seedlings

cabbage

capsicum

eggplant

silver beet

SUBTROPICAL & TROPICAL ZONES

SUBTROPICAL & TROPICAL ZONES

vegetables . . . seed
melon*
onion, white*
pumpkin*
radish*
silver beet
sweetcorn*
zucchini*

*Seed of these plants is best sown straight into the garden. Others should be sown in containers for transplanting later, or may be available now as seedlings.

other jobs for february

- Check suitability of your area for bulbs, and plan accordingly.
- Water garden as the laws for your area permit.
- Sow parsley seed and keep it moist (it may take a few weeks to germinate).
- Plant herbs in pots and keep them moist.
- Stake shallow-rooted shrubs against high winds.
- Maintain deep mulches to minimise runoff.
- Prune poinsettia for sturdier growth (but avoid its poisonous sap).
- Check plants for powdery mildew – a white coating on stems and

leaves (spray with benomyl if necessary).
- Water in citrus fertiliser around papaw and all citrus trees.
- Hand-pollinate pumpkins, melons and other cucurbits if excessive heat or rain is preventing fruit-set.
- Do not allow tomato plants to dry out. Tie up tall varieties before they sprawl.
- Plant a quick-growing climber for the pergola – the red passion flower, *Passiflora coccinea*, perhaps, or one of the cultivars of golden trumpet (*Allamanda cathartica*).
- Plant sweet potatoes in the vegetable garden.
- Lay snailbait after rain.

looking good up north
- Tall white flowerheads on the native river lily (*Crinum pedunculatum*)
- The Brazilian climber *Stigmaphyllon ciliatum*, with orchid-like yellow flowers; the bleeding heart vine (*Clerodendrum thomsonae*), with crimson and white flowers
- Crimson pea flowers on the cockscomb coral tree (*Erythrina crista-galli*); the golden rain tree (*Koelreuteria paniculate*), with sprays of yellow flowers

taking cuttings

Many plants will grow from softwood cuttings.

- Prepare containers and mixture as for seed-raising.
- Choose tips of tender green stems (without flowers) or cut into 5–8 cm lengths. Remove all but a few leaves at top. Dip base in hormone powder (optional).
- Press cuttings, two-thirds buried, into damp mix (as many as you like in one container). Firm well.
- Water, then place container in a large plastic bag held clear of cuttings by sticks.
- Put in shade and keep moist.
- Transfer cuttings to individual pots once roots form (you should check after two weeks).
- Plant out in autumn or spring, or when cuttings have grown to about 15 cm.

Semi-hardwood cuttings, made from older wood, form roots more slowly than softwood cuttings.

Hardwood cuttings do not need special soil or care. They are generally taken from deciduous shrubs or trees, and each piece can be up to 30 cm long. Sink the cuttings about two-thirds deep into the soil, and allow a few months for roots to develop before you plant them out.

SUBTROPICAL & TROPICAL ZONES

march

a month for planting bulbs

JOB FILE

- *Plan April planting of trees, shrubs and climbers*
- *Order roses and fruit trees for winter planting*
- *Start to dig summer mulches into soil*
- *Identify good-looking deciduous trees*
- *Rake up fallen leaves for garden beds and compost*
- *Remove rotting fruit from under trees and destroy it*

It's time to begin planting bulbs for spring flowering (see page 112 for summer-flowering and autumn-flowering bulbs). Many of the plants we call bulbs actually grow from underground organs such as corms (gladiolus, sparaxis), tubers (dahlia, gloxinia) and rhizomes (bearded iris, canna). True bulbs include daffodils, hyacinths, liliums and tulips.

These very desirable plants all have the following characteristics:

- a dormant time, when they have disappeared underground
- a comparatively short but spectacular flowering season
- a bulb-restoration interval after blooming, with leaves left uncut until they dry off
- versatility (suitable for pots, clumps, or mass planting in the case of species like daffodils)
- considerable resilience to diseases and pests
- little need for attention of any kind.

what sort of climate?

The widest range of bulbs grows in relatively cool parts of Australia:

- the south-eastern corner of Western Australia
- the Adelaide Plains, the Mount Lofty Ranges, and the south-east of South Australia
- Tasmania
- most of Victoria
- the east coast of Australia as far north as the elevated country around Brisbane.

Heat and humidity suit comparatively few of the species that flourish in these regions.

what kind of soil?

Good loam rich in humus is required for bulb-growing. Add compost if your soil is not friable, and use fertiliser if it is impoverished.

Drainage must be adequate if rot is to be avoided at wet times.

popular bulbs for spring

The easy-going *Narcissus* family (daffodils and jonquils) comes in a great array of shapes and sizes; spring begins in late winter for some species and cultivars. Once planted they can stay put for many years. Most of the following bulbs are also happy to stay in one place for years.

- Clivia: apricot or cream clusters on stems to 60 cm tall; prefers shade; favours temperate to subtropical areas.
- Grape hyacinth: mostly blue, with tiny bells at the tip of stems 15–24 cm tall; fragrant.
- Iris: bearded, Dutch, Louisiana and so on – all different.
- Ranunculus: in bright yellow, red, pink or white, on stems around 30 cm tall; need lifting in early summer for replanting in autumn.

Note that the pretty little blue *Ipheion uniflora*, often called the star flower, is so easy to grow that it can take over your whole garden.

less common bulbs for spring

The following are attractive and easy to grow.

- Arab's eye lily (*Ornithogalum arabicum*): sweet-scented and white, with waxy black centres; flower clusters that top 40 cm leafless stems.
- Jacobean lily: long-lasting and vivid red, on stems 30–45 cm tall; plant in May, anywhere in Australia.
- Squill: several blue species, with flowers in rosettes; prefers semi-shade.
- Solomon's seal: pendulous green-tipped white bells on stems to 1.5 m or more; needs cool conditions.

planting tips

Ensure that you have chosen the best position for the bulbs you fancy, and lightly dig your organically fortified soil.

Read the bulb supplier's instructions – particularly with regard to depth – and fertilise the soil as recommended (or work in a pinch of slow-release fertiliser about 5 cm below the base of each bulb).

Firm the soil well over the bulbs as you plant them, and water lightly. Further watering will be necessary only in times of drought, but you should keep the area weeded so that you can see the leaves emerge after a few weeks.

cool & temperate zones

Bulb suppliers (a number of them located in Victoria) will send you their catalogues if you want varieties unavailable in nurseries and supermarkets. The more unusual bulbs are sometimes offered in the classified ads of garden magazines. If the weather is dry and hot, wait for rain before planting your bulbs: most can go in any time between March and May.

COOL & TEMPERATE ZONES

flowers to plant

Seed	*Seedlings*
alyssum	ageratum
cineraria	carnation
columbine	forget-me-not
cornflower*	lupin
forget-me-not	pansy
gypsophila*	penstemon
larkspur*	perennial salvia
linaria*	portulaca
lobelia*	stock
love-in-the-mist*	viola
lupin	wallflower
mignonette*	
pansy	
sweet pea*	
Virginian stock*	
wallflower	

vegetables to plant

Seed	*Seedlings*
bean, broad*	broccoli
broccoli	cabbage
cabbage	cauliflower
lettuce*	celery
onion, white*	leek
spinach	silver beet
radish*	
turnip	

*Seed of these plants is best sown straight into the garden. Others should be sown in containers for transplanting later, or may be available now as seedlings.

other jobs for march

- Start a compost heap or bin.
- Tidy finished liliums, and add dead stalks and leaves to compost.
- Dust young cabbage plants, and others in the same family, with derris to deter cabbage moths and butterflies.
- Check plants for scale and spray with white oil if necessary.
- Pick pumpkins, with 5 cm stems, for a few days of weathering before storage.

COOL & TEMPERATE ZONES

- Prepare ground for autumn-sown lawns by raking off stones and other rubbish, then rotary-hoeing, then raking smooth; spray emerging weeds with glyphosate (see page 48 for details and next steps in preparation for lawns).
- Choose positions for new fruit trees, and order for winter planting.
- Prune geraniums hard if you have not already done so.
- Spray affected trees with pyrethrum (according to directions on container) if slimy black pear and cherry slug is active on leaves; or try hosing them off instead. Sprinkling with talcum powder works well for a small area.
- Visit autumn rose shows to inspire your winter planting.
- Stake dahlias, chrysanthemums and Easter daisies if they are starting to sprawl.

looking good down south

- Pumpkins ready to pick
- Dahlias in many colours; Easter daisies in white, blue–mauve, pink, crimson; Japanese anemones, with globular buds and white or pink flowers
- Berrying shrubs (crataegus, pyracantha) and ornamental fruit trees (crab-apples) full of gorgeous and gorging parrots

- The leaves of the pin oak (*Quercus palustris*) and the tulip tree (*Liriodendron tulipifera*) starting to turn; the English oak (*Quercus robur*) weighed down with acorns

the autumn bonus

The highlands of several states as well as the southern parts of Australia suit deciduous trees best. Plant them in winter but notice them now. Here is a choice trio.

- *Acer palmatum* (Japanese maple)

   This smallish tree can grow to about 5 m and has finely cut leaves that are a delicate green in early spring and russet or red in autumn. Very special cultivars like 'Dissectum' need a protected position.

- *Amelanchier canadensis* (shadbush)

   The shadbush may reach 8 m. It has white spring flowers as well as some autumn drama when its foliage turns rusty red.

- *Crataegus phaenopyrum* (Washington thorn)

   This tree grows to 5 m or more and fairly glows when its leaves respond to the changing season. Beware of its long, sharp thorns. There will be autumn berries if the birds spare them.

COOL & TEMPERATE ZONES

subtropical & tropical zones

Since a period of cold weather is essential to the flowering of bulbs such as daffodils and hyacinths, there are many gardens north of Brisbane where these will not do well. Tulips and liliums will grow and flower only in elevated areas.

Certain bulbs, including crinums, grape hyacinths, day lilies (*Hemerocallis* species) and the red nerine (*Nerine sarniensis*), will thrive if given a shady spot.

Reliable ones for all but extreme conditions are agapanthus, belladonnas, clivias, dahlias, freesias, gladiolus, hippeastrums, Jacobean lilies, ranunculus and watsonias. Local specialists should be able to suggest a number of other worthwhile bulbs that suit your area.

flowers to plant

Seed	*Seedlings*
ageratum	ageratum
alyssum	aster
cornflower*	celosia
dianthus	coleus
English daisy*	salvia
Iceland poppy*	sunflower
linaria*	torenia
Livingstone daisy*	
lobelia*	
lupin	
pansy	
salvia	
stock	
sunflower	
sweet pea*	
viola	
Virginian stock*	

SUBTROPICAL & TROPICAL ZONES

SUBTROPICAL & TROPICAL ZONES

vegetables to plant

Seed

bean, French*
beetroot*
broccoli
cabbage
capsicum
carrot*
cauliflower
celery
cucumber*
eggplant
lettuce*
marrow*
onion, white*
pea*
radish*
silver beet
zucchini*

Seedlings

capsicum
cauliflower
celery
eggplant
silver beet

*Seed of these plants is best sown straight into the garden. Others should be sown in containers for transplanting later, or may be available now as seedlings.

other jobs for march

- Start a compost heap or bin (see page 63).
- Dust young cabbage plants, and others in the same family, with derris to deter cabbage moths and butterflies.
- Plant potatoes in the vegetable garden.
- Pick pumpkins, with 5 cm stems, for a few days of weathering before storage.
- Replenish soil leached by summer downpours: add compost, fertiliser and dolomite.
- Plant mangoes and a clump of papaws.
- Consider planting avocados, bananas, custard apples, lychees, macadamias, sapodillas and star fruits – preferably in spring.
- Check garden for its range of plants. Are there enough small species such as ferns filling the gaps between shrubs and trees?
- Take more cuttings, including leaf cuttings of African violets, rex begonias, gloxinias and peperomias: insert half-leaves into potting mix with veins pointing downwards (roots will form at ends of veins).
- Tidy herbs by weeding them and removing dried stems and leaves. Sprinkle half a handful of complete fertiliser around each.

SUBTROPICAL & TROPICAL ZONES

looking good up north

- Amaranthus, coleus, torenia
- Hibiscus in brilliant red, pink and orange shades
- The umbrella tree (*Schefflera actinophylla*), with striking red flower spikes; the Hong Kong orchid tree (*Bauhinia blakeana*), with fragrant carmine flowers
- Striking red flowers against glossy leaves on the firewheel tree (*Stenocarpus sinuatus*)

strawberry-planting time

In subtropical and tropical areas it is time to renovate old strawberry beds and establish fresh ones. The varieties Earlisweet and Redlands Crimson will begin to produce crops in June or July.

Old beds:

- Weed; remove dead leaves and excess runners.
- Mulch with well-rotted animal manure or good compost, then cover that with clean hay.

New beds:

- Buy virus-free plants of a locally available variety.
- Dig compost into the chosen bed.
- Mark planting spots about 30 cm apart, work in a generous pinch of complete fertiliser, and cover with about 5 cm of soil.

- Plant crowns firmly and water well.
- Tuck thick wads of clean straw or hay close to plants and over all bare soil.

In cool and temperate parts of Australia all this work should be done at about the same time, but the rewards will not come until summer.

SUBTROPICAL & TROPICAL ZONES

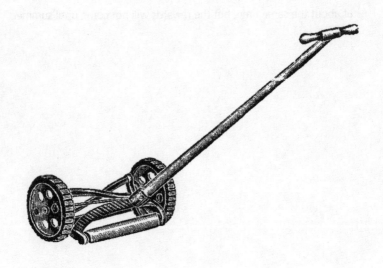

april

a month for lawn care

JOB FILE

- *Have an autumn clean-up*
- *Continue planting bulbs*
- *Choose evergreen trees, shrubs and climbers for planting after rain*
- *Plant flower and vegetable seedlings from January and February container sowings*
- *Do last big sowing for spring flowers and crops*
- *Divide and replant perennials, and buy new ones*
- *Fertilise fruit trees*
- *Spray deciduous fruit trees with Bordeaux mixture and white oil as leaves fall*

In southern parts of Australia autumn is a good time to start a lawn (spring is another). Conditions in Perth, Adelaide, Melbourne and Sydney are unlikely to offer new lawns too many setbacks (provided there is sufficient rain), and in places like Canberra and Hobart the grass will be well established before winter brings growth to a halt. On the subtropical and tropical coasts, however, lawns are best planted between September and February. Even though the mild, dry, northern winter encourages many plants to flower, new lawns do not seem to thrive at that time – they simply sulk and wait for spring.

April is a month when lawns everywhere will benefit from some extra attention. You can tackle weeds with an old knife, or spray the lawn with a selective herbicide. Ideally lawns should be watered thoroughly and only twice a week to toughen the grass and encourage deep roots. Check your local water-usage rules to see when you are permitted to water your lawn.

do you need a lawn?

A lawn is no longer the key feature of every Australian garden (many people prefer wood chips, paving stones, pressed sand or hardy groundcovers to grass), but it is hard to beat as a pleasant sitting and playing area for families throughout the year. As a landscape element it often has an important role in tying other parts of the garden together. However, lawns are water-guzzlers so consider keeping grassy areas to a minimum.

Rough grass can be mown regularly to produce an informal lawn, and that may be all you require. The Australian ground-hugger kidneyweed (*Dichondra repens*), now available in seed form, makes a soft green carpet of kidney-shaped leaves and suits many parts of the country. A 'real' lawn takes more effort to establish and maintain.

preparation

Allow at least a month for preparation, whether you are going to sow seed, plant offsets or put down instant turf.

- Check drainage: create a slight fall on flat sites, or lay drainage pipes if necessary.
- Rake stones and other rubbish off the chosen area.
- Rotary-hoe or dig to a depth of about 15 cm, then rake smooth.
- Water as your local laws permit, and allow weeds to come up for a couple of weeks.
- Spray weeds with a herbicide containing glyphosate and wait another fortnight.
- Rake out dead weeds and re-rake until the surface of the soil is fine and smooth.

sowing lawn seed

Most gardeners in the subtropical and tropical north grow their lawns from offsets or instant turf, but Queensland blue couch or Indian green couch may be established there from seed, as the grasses most popular in the southern states generally are. The following is the procedure for sowing in either spring (preferred in the north) or autumn.

- Consult local suppliers on the best seed for your district and requirements. Buy more than the quantity per square metre recommended by the seed firm.

- Divide the seed into two parts and broadcast, the first half in one direction and the second at right angles to it.
- Run a light roller over the area (or press down with a home-made rammer).
- Water lightly, and keep moist throughout dry weather as much as your local laws permit.
- Set mower blades high for the first cut, mowing when grass is thick and 5–8 cm high.

planting offsets ('sprigs')

This method of growing lawn, the normal one in Queensland, is confined in southern states to varieties for which seed is unavailable. The offsets are pressed into well-prepared damp soil (about 30 cm apart) and kept moist until they root. In the north this is always done in spring.

laying instant lawn

Instantaneous green is what you get from rolls of pre-grown turf, which are laid edge to edge and watered thoroughly and frequently until the grass takes hold. This is the most costly option, but a worthwhile one provided you have prepared the ground thoroughly and do not stint the watering at any stage. In some states you may need a permit to water your new turf.

cool & temperate zones

Gardeners in Perth and Adelaide, cities that in summer normally experience high temperatures and the lowest rainfall of all state capitals, should make sure that the lawns they plant can stand such conditions without constant pampering.

flowers to plant

Seed	*Seedlings*
alyssum	ageratum
cineraria	alyssum
columbine	Canterbury bell
cornflower*	carnation
forget-me-not	cineraria
gypsophila*	columbine
larkspur*	forget-me-not

flowers . . . seed
linaria*
lobelia*
love-in-the-mist*
lupin
Shirley poppy*
sweet pea*
Virginian stock*
wallflower

flowers . . . seedlings
lupin
pansy
penstemon
perennial salvia
petunia
stock
viola
wallflower

vegetables to plant

Seed
bean, broad*
cabbage
cauliflower
celery
lettuce*
onion (midseason)
silver beet
spinach

Seedlings
broccoli
cabbage
cauliflower
celery
silver beet

COOL & TEMPERATE ZONES

*Seed of these plants is best sown straight into the garden. Others should be sown
in containers for transplanting later, or may be available now as seedlings.

a perennial chore

Flowering perennials such as acanthus, heuchera, delphinium, rudbeckia and shasta daisy are an easy-going lot, but once a year they need a little attention. Check yours now.

- Have they finished flowering? If so, remove dry stems and yellow leaves. If not, postpone action until they are dormant.
- Do they need dividing? The plants themselves will tell you by losing vigour or pushing their crowns out of the ground. You may want to confine them anyway. If they don't need dividing, work a handful of blood and bone into the soil round each.

Dividing and replanting is easiest on a cool day after rain.

- Prepare new ground, incorporating compost and a little blood and bone.
- Cut off three-quarters of the growth.
- Dig out the whole clump and select rooted offsets from the outside of the clump. Discard the rest.
- Plant the offsets firmly in their new position and water well. Maintain watering, if conditions are dry, until plants are well established.

other jobs for april

- Add fallen leaves to compost bin or heap.

COOL & TEMPERATE ZONES

- Dust young cabbage plants, and others in the same family, with derris to deter cabbage moths and butterflies.
- Choose positions for new fruit trees, and order for winter planting.
- Notice emerging nerines, and resolve to plant some white ones in February or March for Mother's Day next year.
- Rake gypsum into excessively clayey soils at the rate of two or three cups per square metre.
- Water mature fruit trees well, fork holes around their dripline, and cover holes with two or three buckets of dry poultry manure. Alternatively, pour into holes a mixture of complete fertiliser and sulphate of ammonia (1 kg complete fertiliser and 300 g sulphate of ammonia per tree); water again.
- Lift some lilium bulbs if plants have become overcrowded. Choose firm, medium-size ones to replant (as soon as possible) in good, well-prepared soil.
- Lift corms of finished gladiolus. Discard shrivelled parts and store plump corms in a cool, dry place.

looking good down south

- Chrysanthemums – all sizes and colours; white and pink nerines
- Bottlebrushes (especially forms of *Callistemon citrinus*) in a second flush of bloom

COOL & TEMPERATE ZONES

- The rangy Madeira vine (*Anredera cordifolia*) sprouting long, fragrant chains of tiny cream flowers
- The rose sheoak (*Allocasuarina torulosa*) glowing with tiny flowers

subtropical & tropical zones

Wherever you live, locally recommended types of lawn are the most likely to do well, though the suggestion of kikuyu for cooler parts of the north should be resisted because of its invasiveness.

Queensland blue couch and the Indian green couch are widely grown in subtropical regions (usually from sprigs planted September–February), and narrow-leaved carpet grass is also useful. Further north, broad-leaved carpet grass makes a good lawn that will flourish all year round; it is always grown from sprigs or instant turf because seed is not available commercially.

Though spring and early summer are the best times for planting lawns in the north, lawn improvement can be tackled now, as in other parts of Australia. Weed and fertilise the grass – a complete fertiliser low in nitrogen is best at this time of year. Water after fertilising, observing the water-usage rules for your area.

flowers to plant

Seed	*Seedlings*
ageratum	ageratum
alyssum	celosia
cornflower*	coleus
dianthus	lupin
English daisy*	pansy
larkspur*	salvia
linaria*	sunflower
Livingstone daisy*	viola
lobelia*	
lupin	
pansy	
petunia	
salvia	
stock	
sunflower	
sweet pea*	
verbena	
viola	

SUBTROPICAL & TROPICAL ZONES

SUBTROPICAL & TROPICAL ZONES

vegetables to plant

Seed	*Seedlings*
bean, French*	cabbage
beetroot*	capsicum
broccoli	cauliflower
cabbage	celery
carrot*	eggplant
cauliflower	silver beet
celery	tomato
cucumber*	
leek	
lettuce*	
melon	
pea*	
pumpkin*	
radish*	
silver beet	
spinach	
tomato	
zucchini*	

*Seed of these plants is best sown straight into the garden. Others should be sown in containers for transplanting later, or may be available now as seedlings.

other jobs for april

- Add garden refuse, including dead fern fronds, to compost.
- Dust young cabbage plants, and others in the same family, with derris to deter cabbage moths and butterflies.
- Plant shade trees, replacements for trees lost in summer storms and cyclones, and any other trees, shrubs or climbers (include fruiting or ornamental passionfruit if wanted).
- Choose a cool day after rain for lifting and dividing perennials.
- Take side shoots of bromeliads to replace old stock. Plant shoots in a shady corner with well-drained soil.
- Check lawns for the fungal disease dollar spot (cobwebby brown patches) and spray with triadimefon or benomyl if necessary.
- Give roses a boost with fertiliser, to encourage further flowering.
- Fertilise flowering hibiscus and renew mulches around all plants.
- Lift a drab part of the garden by adding three or four shrimp plants, which will provide a display of unusual pinkish bracts and tiny white flowers almost continuously.
- Plant potatoes and shallots in the vegetable garden.
- Pick persimmons when they have reached and held their brightest orange colour but are still firm; soften completely indoors before eating.
- Plant gladiolus corms: choose a well-drained, sunny spot in enriched soil.

SUBTROPICAL & TROPICAL ZONES

looking good up north

- Dahlias in many colours; Easter daisies in white, blue-mauve, pink, crimson
- Two small shrubs: *Ixora coccinea*, with starry red flowers; *Gardenia jasminoides*, with fragrant double white flowers
- Deep orange persimmons mingling with the orange and red leaves on the tree
- Autumn foliage (reddish orange) against the cinnamon trunks of crepe myrtle (*Lagerstroemia indica*)

liquid refreshment

Plants need frequent nourishment, just as people do, and soluble fertilisers applied by watering-can are the equivalent of a healthy snack. Although fertilisers of this kind cannot take the place of the slower-acting chemical compounds dug into the soil, they are valuable and quick-acting stimulants to growth.

If you have farm manure on hand and time to spare, you will find that home-made liquid fertiliser is an effective substitute for the commercial product. This is how to make it:

- Place a large rubbish bin near a tap but not too close to the house.
- Tie a knot at the top of each leg of a pair of pantyhose. Stuff the top part with fresh manure and tie the waist securely.

- Fill the bin with water. Drop in the 'bag' of manure but let the legs hang out over the edge of the bin. Clip the lid on.
- Using the dangling pantyhose legs as handles, shake the bag of manure in the water every day for a week or so.
- Before sprinkling the liquid onto your well-established plants, dilute it to the colour of weak tea; make it weaker for seedlings.
- Refill the bin with water, and shake the bag again, for repeated doses; each batch will be weaker than the last and eventually no diluting will be needed.

SUBTROPICAL & TROPICAL ZONES

may

a month for a making compost

JOB FILE

- *Plant citrus trees in warm districts*
- *Remove autumn-flowering annuals as they finish*
- *Plant ornamental evergreen trees, shrubs and climbers in all districts*
- *Trim autumn-flowering shrubs as they fade*
- *Plant flower and vegetable seedlings from February and March container sowings*
- *Divide and replant perennials, and buy new ones*

Don't discard that garden debris – compost it! Compost-making is a job for every day of the year and every Australian garden, but leaf-fall in the southern states often prompts an autumn start. Once you realise that those untidy heaps of oak, beech, ash and poplar leaves can be combined with other house and garden debris to improve your soil enormously, you'll learn to love them.

what is compost?

Compost is a soil-improver consisting of decomposed organic materials, principally discarded vegetable matter and animal manure.

why bother?

Gardens that get lots of compost grow better than those that
don't. This is because compost adds humus to the soil, and soil rich
in humus has a structure that retains moisture well, allows air to
penetrate to the roots, and helps plants to absorb the nutrients they
need. Some compost is itself a source of nutrients.

A compost bin or heap is also a great recycling machine, a highly
productive way to dispose of kitchen and garden waste.

what equipment is necessary?

Go for the composting set-up that best suits your circumstances.

- If your garden is small, buy a compost bin, preferably one with
  airholes in the sides.
- For a medium-size garden you'll need at least a couple of
  commercial bins, or a home-made structure of timber, brick or wire
  netting.
- Very large gardens need vast amounts of compost and have room
  for several composting areas.

When you buy your bin or build the housing for your heap, bear in
mind the three essentials for composting:

- organic matter that will rot down over a few months
- moisture, but not too much of it

- oxygen that can penetrate all parts of the compost.

suitable organic matter

The following are among the possibilities:

- kitchen refuse (excluding meat, which attracts vermin, but including eggshells, peelings, tea leaves and coffee grounds, and dampened scrap paper)
- garden rubbish (weeds without seedheads, pulled annuals, lawn clippings, light prunings and fallen leaves)
- animal manure (horse, cow, poultry and so on).

You may also add hay, seaweed (with thick kelp chopped up), pre-loved commercial mushroom compost, anything woody that has gone through a shredder, and (in small quantities only) sawdust, wood shavings and pine needles. Degraded soil is useful too.

Although heat from the decomposing material should kill weed seeds and plant-borne diseases, it is often suggested that gardeners play safe by excluding seedheads and any obviously diseased material.

moisture control

It is easier to check the moisture level of compost heaps than of the commercial bins, whose contents are less accessible. Neither should ever be really dry, or saturated for long periods. Open heaps may have to be covered from time to time in cold, wet weather.

access for oxygen

Decomposition cannot take place if oxygen is excluded. Bins should
have pierced sides, and home-built structures need slits in brickwork,
gaps between planks.

Compost should be stirred and turned from time to time to mix the
ingredients, and this helps aeration. Lawn clippings are particularly
prone to packing down unless incorporated thoroughly.

composting kept simple

It is possible to compost scientifically, balancing the chemistry so that
you turn out a soil-improver of considerable fertility. Most people
get good results from a more straightforward procedure, however,
especially if they have two bins (or a divided structure), to allow for
compost at different stages and therefore a continuous supply.

- First buy your bin or build your structure, siting it away from the
  house if possible.
- For every 30 cm or so of new vegetable matter thrown in, add
  a thin layer of something that can help the rotting process: old
  compost, animal manure or commercial mushroom compost, and
  an occasional handful of blood and bone or sulphate of ammonia.

Top it off with a few shovelfuls of soil, however poor.
- Add whatever comes to hand, whenever it comes.
- Stir your bin or turn over your heap at least once a month, and
keep the contents moist.

The compost is ready to use when it has rotted into a dark, fibrous
mass – after four to six months in the cooler parts of the continent,
sooner in the warmer regions. Use it as a mulch around plants, or dig
it lightly into the topsoil.

cool & temperate zones

The deciduous ornamentals of the southern states – ash, beech, birch,
elm, oak and poplar, for example – can contribute greatly to well-
balanced compost. Some of the fallen leaves should be left where
they lie to nourish the ground naturally, but all the excess can go into
your bin or heap. Leaves are often slow to rot, however; if possible
they should be put through a shredder first, or even just have the
mower run over them.

flowers to plant

Seed	*Seedlings*
alyssum	ageratum
cineraria	alyssum
forget-me-not	carnation
larkspur*	cineraria
lupin	columbine
Shirley poppy*	forget-me-not
Virginian stock*	lupin
	pansy
	penstemon
	perennial salvia
	polyanthus
	primrose
	viola
	wallflower

vegetables to plant

Seed	*Seedlings*
bean, broad*	cabbage
cabbage	celery

COOL & TEMPERATE ZONES

COOL & TEMPERATE ZONES

vegetables . . . seed
cauliflower
onion (midseason
    and late)
pea*
spinach

vegetables . . . seedlings
leek
onion (midseason
    and late)
silver beet
spinach
turnip

*Seed of these plants is best sown straight into the garden. Others should be sown in containers for transplanting later, or may be available now as seedlings.

other jobs for may

- Dig over and mound up soil for planting of new citrus (in frost-free areas) and ornamental evergreen trees (see 'Planting citrus' on page 75).
- Cut asparagus foliage to the ground and add it to compost.
- Lift and divide perennial flowers. Replant offsets in good soil.
- Remove dead leaves and runners from old strawberry beds and mulch plants with rotted manure or compost. Plant new strawberries in good soil and mulch with straw and hay.
- Cut finished raspberry canes, and weak new ones, to the ground.
- Take hardwood cuttings of deciduous plants (15–30 cm long) and insert in garden soil. Those that 'take' can be moved next autumn.

- Deadhead autumn bulbs as they finish, but do not cut stems or leaves until they dry off.
- Cut finished herbs to the ground. Feed parsley with liquid fertiliser.
- Trim dead foliage from kangaroo paws: divide plants if you want new ones.
- Plant new liliums.

looking good down south

- Autumn-sown lettuce hearting up nicely
- Sasanqua camellias in bloom, the ground carpeted with petals; Payne's thryptomene crowded with tiny pink flowers
- Heavily fruiting cumquats
- The Irish strawberry tree (*Arbutus unedo*), its waxy white flowers falling and its large orange–red fruits forming

choice shrubs for southern gardens

A clump of small Australian shrubs could include several of each of the following.

- *Astartea fascicularis* (astartea)
  Delicate foliage, and dainty white flowers most of the year, are features of this slender shrub, commonly 1–2.5 m tall.

COOL & TEMPERATE ZONES

- *Boronia pinnata* (pinnate boronia)
  The feathery leaflets and neat form of the metre-tall pinnate boronia make it attractive all year round. Clusters of starry pink flowers appear in spring.
- *Calytrix sullivanii* (calytrix)
  Put this shrub (2–4 m tall) in a well-drained, semi-shaded position and it will bloom reliably in late spring; the little flowers are white to palest pink.
- *Eriostemon verrucosus* (fairy wax-flower)
  There are various forms of the fairy wax-flower in a range of sizes; most forms flower prolifically, and have pink buds opening to white flowers in winter–spring.

All four shrubs benefit from tip-pruning as they grow, and clipping over after they have finished flowering.

subtropical & tropical zones

In northern Australian gardens compost rots down speedily. Take advantage of composting opportunities, because soil is regularly washed away or leached of nutrients in these regions. Pile compost high on beds to help reduce runoff. You will not need to cover open heaps after extensive summer rain: the warmth will get decomposition going again.

flowers to plant

Seed	*Seedlings*
ageratum	ageratum
alyssum	alyssum
cornflower*	dianthus
dianthus	lupin
English daisy*	pansy
larkspur*	salvia
linaria*	stock
Livingstone daisy*	sunflower
lobelia*	viola

SUBTROPICAL & TROPICAL ZONES

flowers . . . seed
lupin
pansy
petunia
phlox*
portulaca
salvia
stock
sunflower
sweet pea*
viola

vegetables to plant

Seed	*Seedlings*
bean, French*	broccoli
beetroot*	cabbage
broccoli	capsicum
cabbage	cauliflower
carrot*	celery
cucumber*	eggplant
leek	silver beet
lettuce*	tomato

vegetables . . . seed
melon*
onion (midseason)
pea*
pumpkin*
radish*
silver beet
spinach
tomato
zucchini*

SUBTROPICAL & TROPICAL ZONES

*Seed of these plants is best sown straight into the garden. Others should be sown in containers for transplanting later, or may be available now as seedlings.

other jobs for may

- Sow a 'green manure' crop (lupin, vetch, broad bean) in a vacant bed to add nitrogen and humus to the soil. Dig it in just before it flowers, and plant vegetables six weeks later.
- Plant peanuts in dry areas with sandy soil.
- Plant some garlic.
- Cut asparagus foliage to the ground and add it to compost. Plant new beds of two-year-old asparagus crowns, using rich soil.
- Lime soil well before planting beans and peas.

- Weed strawberry plants thoroughly, and sprinkle with liquid fertiliser every fortnight or so.
- Plant passionfruit vines.
- Deadhead autumn bulbs as they finish, but do not cut stems or leaves until they dry off.
- Plant potatoes and shallots in the vegetable garden.
- Add a flame vine (*Pyrostegia venusta*) to the garden (on a fence or pergola) for striking colour in late autumn and winter.
- Prepare planting places for new roses and fruit trees ordered earlier. Never plant a new rose where a diseased rose has been.
- Plant gladiolus corms and, if the weather is dry, water the plants as they emerge and grow.
- Plant ranunculus and anemone roots, with a little sand under each.
- Take cuttings of conifers (use three parts of sand, one part of peat moss).
- Try herb cuttings – they grow quicker than seed in warm climates.

looking good up north

- Angelwing jasmine (*Jasminum nitidum*), a scrambling groundcover displaying fragrant white flowers
- The small native shrub *Calytrix exstipulata*, with star-like pale-pink flowers

- The flame vine (*Pyrostegia venusta*), with red and orange tubular flowers
- The exotic frangipani (*Plumeria rubra*), with sweet-smelling cream, pink, apricot or red flowers

planting citrus

Citrus trees may be planted in northern gardens between May and September (later in frost-prone areas). Choose locally recommended varieties of lemon, orange, mandarin, grapefruit and lime, all of which need good drainage and a sunny position.

Prepare the site a couple of weeks ahead.

- Dig a hole about 45 cm wide and 30 cm deep, working in several handfuls of dolomite if the soil is acid.
- Refill the hole and build a mound at least 30 cm high over it, using compost or other good soil.

Plant the tree as follows:

- Open up the mound and fill with water.
- Insert the tree so that its budding union (a bulge near the base) is well above ground level. Spread the roots carefully.
- Cover the roots with soil, firm down and water deeply. Mulch thickly to suppress weeds.

june

a month for deciduous plants

JOB FILE

- *Check moisture content of compost bin or heap*
- *Smother weeds with thick mulch*
- *Divide and replant perennials, and buy new ones*
- *Plant flower and vegetable seedlings from March and April container sowings*
- *Take hardwood cuttings*
- *Do a midyear stocktake of the garden*
- *Catch up with garden books and magazines*

Give some thought this month to deciduous plants – those that lose their leaves at the end of the growing season. Even in subtropical regions the reduced temperatures of autumn cause leaf-fall in this kind of plant, but northern conditions usually lack the period of real chilliness that produces striking colour-change.

By June the autumn showiness of the Adelaide Hills, southern Victoria, Tasmania, Canberra and parts of the New South Wales Highlands is over, but many people like the leafless phase too. Shapely trunks and branches certainly become more apparent then.

Now is the time to begin planting deciduous trees, shrubs and climbers, and to prune and spray deciduous fruit trees.

planting

Deciduous plants are heavily stocked by nurseries in winter, and many (including fruit trees and roses) are sold bare-rooted. This means that roots have had no chance to curl round and round, as they sometimes do when confined. You may need to tease out the roots if your plants have been in pots for some time.

Once you have decided what you want and where it is to go, prepare the ground immediately. Note that all evergreens except those likely to be frostbitten can also be planted at this time of year. The procedure is the same as for deciduous species.

- Dig a patch about 30 cm deep and at least 45 cm wide. If this depth takes you into hard clay, stop digging and plan to build a mound above ground level to achieve 30 cm of friable loam. Fruit trees in particular need a mound to grow in, for good drainage.
- Mix old, broken-up animal manure or good-quality compost through the soil. Two or three cups of gypsum will help to free up hard ground.
- Plant a couple of weeks later, first soaking bare-rooted plants for half an hour and watering any potted stock.
- Fill the planting hole with water and let it drain.
- Throw a couple of handfuls of blood and bone into the hole and cover it with a shovelful of loam.

- Hold the stem straight and spread the roots wide as you push in the soil and mound it up. Keep any budding or grafting bulge above ground level.
- Press the earth firmly into place and water well.

winter spraying

Established deciduous fruit trees need at least a couple of winter sprayings to control various fungal diseases, mites, scales and aphids. Peaches usually require spraying against leaf curl. Your apples and pears are very likely to be affected by codling and light brown apple moth unless you are prepared to spray repeatedly.

Spray all deciduous fruit trees now with Bordeaux mixture or copper oxychloride and, at the end of July, with dormant oil.

winter pruning

- Shape deciduous ornamental trees and shrubs now; remove criss-crossing branches. Roses should not be pruned until July, however.
- Cut back deciduous fruit trees to control their size, to produce the right amount of fruit-bearing wood (for small crops of large fruit), and to stimulate new growth from time to time. Check the requirements of particular types of fruit trees, because they vary.

deciduous ornamental trees to plant

For cool areas:

- *Cornus florida* (dogwood), small tree with white spring flowers and reddish autumn foliage
- *Malus ioensis* 'Plena' (Bechtel's crab-apple), medium tree with fragrant pink flowers in spring and attractive autumn foliage
- *Pistacia chinensis* (Chinese pistachio), small to medium tree with red autumn foliage
- *Quercus coccinea* (scarlet oak), large tree with spectacular red autumn foliage.

For temperate areas:

- *Dais cotinifolia* (South African pompom tree), fast-growing small tree with globular pink summer flowers
- *Liriodendron tulipifera* (tulip tree), lofty tree with unusual greenish spring flowers and golden autumn foliage
- *Prunus mume* 'Alphandii' (Japanese apricot), non-fruiting small tree with sweet-scented pink flowers in early winter
- *Sorbus aucuparia* (rowan), medium tree with white spring flowers, orange–red autumn berries and reddish autumn foliage.

For warm and subtropical areas:

- *Cassia fistula* (golden shower), small tree with clusters of sweet-smelling yellow flowers in summer, followed by long brown pods

- *Diospyros kaki* (persimmon), small to medium tree with orange and red autumn foliage and deep orange fruit (to be ripened indoors) in autumn
- *Erythrina indica* (Indian coral tree), small to medium tree with striking red pea flowers on bare winter branches
- *Lagerstroemia indica* (crepe myrtle), small tree with pink summer flowers and reddish orange autumn foliage.

deciduous ornamental shrubs to plant

For cool areas:

- *Berberis thunbergii* 'Atropurpurea' (Japanese barberry), medium shrub with yellow spring flowers, and purple foliage turning flame-coloured in autumn
- *Cotinus coggygria* (smoke tree), medium to large shrub with smoke-grey clouds of tiny spring flowers, and orange and red autumn foliage
- *Hydrangea quercifolia* (oakleaf hydrangea), medium shrub with creamy spring flowers and interesting, deeply lobed leaves, russet and orange in autumn
- *Kerria japonica* (Japanese rose), medium shrub covered with yellow flowers in spring.

For temperate areas:
- *Deutzia gracilis*, small shrub with clusters of dainty white spring flowers
- *Philadelphus* 'Virginal', large shrub with fragrant late spring flowers and clear yellow autumn foliage
- *Punica granatum* 'Nana' (miniature pomegranate), small shrub with bright-red summer flowers and tiny pomegranates amid pinkish-rust foliage in autumn
- *Viburnum opulus* 'Sterile' (snowball tree), medium shrub with large globular heads of white flowers in spring, and rusty red foliage in autumn.

For warm and subtropical areas:
- *Caesalpinia gilliesii* (bird of paradise), medium shrub with clusters of showy red and yellow flowers in summer and autumn
- *Hibiscus syriacus* (rose of Sharon), medium shrub with small summer flowers in white, pink or blue – no further north than Brisbane
- *Plumeria* species (frangipani), medium to large, fleshy-stemmed shrub with fragrant cream, pink, apricot or red flowers from November to May
- *Spiraea cantoniensis*, medium shrub with white spring flowers and bronze–yellow autumn foliage – no further north than Brisbane.

cool & temperate zones

The choice of deciduous species available to gardeners in the southern states is extensive. Deciduous climbers such as kiwi-fruit, Virginia creeper, wisteria and the exotic clematis species and cultivars can be planted now, like the trees and shrubs. Before you buy, use your references to check the plants you fancy for their soil and moisture requirements, wind tolerance and resistance to pests and diseases.

The smaller deciduous plants are usually sold in pots (rather than bare-rooted). Good stock should not be root-bound at this time of year; use a reliable supplier, and check the pots as you make your choice at the nursery.

Remember that deciduous plants will be dormant until spring and therefore, once settled in, will not need watering unless there is an extended drought.

flowers to plant

Seed	*Seedlings*
alyssum	alyssum
candytuft	cineraria
hollyhock*	columbine
larkspur*	forget-me-not
linaria*	lupin
love-in-the-mist*	wallflower
mignonette*	
stock	

vegetables to plant

Seed	*Seedlings*
bean, broad*	cabbage
cabbage	cauliflower
onion (midseason and late)	celery
pea*	leek
spinach	onion (midseason and late)
	silver beet
	spinach

*Seed of these plants is best sown straight into the garden. Others should be sown in containers for transplanting later, or may be available now as seedlings.

COOL & TEMPERATE ZONES

COOL & TEMPERATE ZONES

other jobs for june

- Sharpen secateurs and saws for winter pruning jobs.
- Reduce watering of house-plants.
- Plant potatoes in New South Wales, South Australia and Western Australia.
- Plant rhubarb crowns in soil enriched with old manure, super-phosphate, and blood and bone. Give established plants a mulch of manure and a dressing of blood and bone.
- Lift and divide perennial flowers. Replant offsets in good soil.
- Check pollination requirements of deciduous fruit trees before you buy; consider multi-grafted trees for interesting combinations of fruit and for cross-pollination.
- Put rotted cow manure under roses at planting time (with soil protecting the roots).
- Erect trellis for raspberries. Mulch plants with compost and manure.
- Attack weeds in lawns.
- Tip-prune young sweet peas.
- Plant geraniums, including ones from February cuttings.
- Plant last of spring bulbs, including tulips and hyacinths.

looking good down south

- Violets, violets, violets!
- *Daphne odora* (the well-known daphne), covered with fragrant waxy pale-pink posies
- Another beautifully scented shrub, allspice (*Chimonanthus praecox*), its perfume coming from interesting small waxy star flowers
- The heath banksia (*Banksia ericifolia*), with tall cones of a striking bronze

drain-blockers

The winter rains of cool and temperate regions always put stormwater drains to the test, and plant roots are often to blame when they fail. Sewage drains are also liable to be clogged in this way. Fine roots sneak into pipes, at first impeding the flow only a little but capable of blocking it entirely.

A product recommended for destroying roots in drains without damaging plants may solve your problems, but more drastic (and expensive) action is sometimes needed. Local councils can usually offer advice, and their lists of the more notorious drain-blockers are likely to include the following:

- ashes, elms, poplars, willows, and all kinds of fig

COOL & TEMPERATE ZONES

- angophoras, eucalypts, large-growing melaleucas, and some callistemons, hakeas and wattles.

subtropical & tropical zones

The range of ornamental deciduous trees, shrubs and climbers that prosper (and colour up) in these zones is limited, but there are now tropical varieties of deciduous fruit trees including apple, pear, nectarine, peach and plum. Also, the lively hues of indigenous and exotic evergreens (to say nothing of the numerous annuals, perennials and climbers on offer) guarantee colour all year round.

flowers to plant

Seed	*Seedlings*
ageratum	ageratum
alyssum	alyssum
cornflower*	dianthus
cosmos	lupin

flowers . . . seed
dianthus
larkspur*
lupin
petunia
phlox*
portulaca
salvia
verbena

flowers . . . seedlings
pansy
petunia
salvia
stock
sunflower
verbena
viola

vegetables to plant

Seed
bean, French*
beetroot*
broccoli
cabbage
carrot*
cucumber*
leek
lettuce*
melon*

Seedlings
broccoli
cabbage
cauliflower
celery
leek
onion (late)
silver beet
spinach
tomato

SUBTROPICAL & TROPICAL ZONES

vegetables . . . seed
onion (late)
pea*
pumpkin*
radish*
silver beet
spinach
tomato
zucchini*

*Seed of these plants is best sown straight into the garden. Others should be sown in containers for transplanting later, or may be available now as seedlings.

other jobs for june

- Apply liquid fertiliser to developing vegetables such as members of the cabbage family, and to all flower seedlings.
- Plant potatoes, sweet potatoes, chives and shallots in the vegetable garden. Mound soil around potatoes already growing, to prevent infestation by the potato moth.
- Plant rhubarb crowns in soil enriched with old manure, super-phosphate, and blood and bone. Give established plants a mulch of manure and a dressing of blood and bone.

- Inquire about recommended varieties of deciduous fruit trees for your area.
- Put rotted cow manure under roses at planting time (with soil protecting the roots).
- Split up clumps of day lily (*Hemerocallis* species) after six or seven years, or if new plants are wanted.
- Attack conspicuous weeds in lawns. Dig any bindii out of lawns now (or spray with a selective herbicide), before seed is dispersed.
- Lift dahlia tubers and store them in sawdust to prevent drying out and rot.
- Plant gladiolus corms.
- Squash caterpillars visible on foliage (rather than spray ones you can't see). Look underneath as well as on top.

looking good up north

- Red-hot pokers; elephant's ear (*Bergenia cordifolia*), with clusters of mid-pink flowers
- The large, fluffy yellow flowerheads of the silver-leaved Mount Morgan wattle (*Acacia podalyriifolia*)
- The showy crimson-scarlet flowers of flame of the forest (*Butea frondosa*)

SUBTROPICAL & TROPICAL ZONES

clean up that scale

Scale is the protective coating laid down by various insects that infest, and can seriously harm, plants such as citrus and other fruit trees, palms, ferns, orchids, roses and eucalypts. Scale insects are active in summer and dormant in winter. At any time of year you may see ants eating the honeydew secreted by the insects, or notice sooty mould on it. Ants should be brushed off and squashed where possible, as they often worsen scale attacks.

You may choose to ignore scale, hoping that natural predators (ladybirds and certain wasps) will control it, or you can intervene. Possible action now:

- Scrub off small patches with a soft toothbrush dipped in diluted white oil (20 ml in a litre of water).
- Spray heavy infestations with white oil at the same rate.
- Cut off and burn badly damaged stems and leaves.

Possible action in summer:

- Spray with white oil (10 ml per litre of water) plus maldison (2 ml per litre of water).

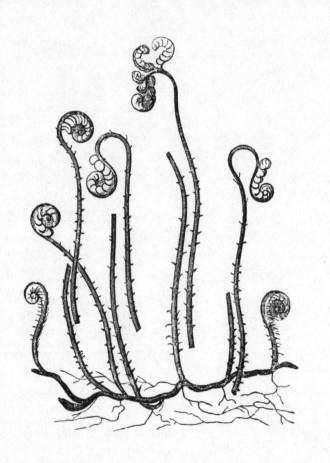

july

a month for garden design

JOB FILE

- *Carry out heavy construction jobs (paving, pergolas, walls, steps)*
- *Continue planting deciduous trees, shrubs and climbers*
- *Plant new roses*
- *Prune roses and deciduous fruit trees*
- *Plant flower and vegetable seedlings from April and May container sowings*
- *Take hardwood cuttings*
- *Spray with white oil any plants heavily affected by scale*

Satisfactory garden design is a happy blend of good looks and practicality, and handsome gardens that fail to meet the needs of their owners are not much better than functional ones lacking in charm. Nowadays a functional garden should also be able to thrive without guzzling large amounts of water. Clever design (with attention paid to plant selection and grouping) can help save water.

Midwinter, when the garden is resting in the south and moving gently in the north, is a suitable time for designing a new garden or redesigning an old one. If the plan involves the construction of paths, steps and other such elements there is time to do it before spring, when you will want to plant as much as possible.

begin where you are

You may have a new building surrounded by a wilderness of clay and builder's rubbish; a neglected house and garden to which you have just shifted; or any other garden in need of a new look and fresh ideas.

What lies behind the fences is also relevant: other houses, commercial premises, or hills and paddocks.

decide what you like

Ask yourself some questions about style.

- What kind of garden is suggested by the house and its setting?
- Do I like formal gardens or informal ones?
- Do I want natives, exotics or a mixture?
- Are my tastes romantic, classical, modern?
- Do I want to fit in with neighbouring gardens or to be different?

decide what you need

Your checklist might include some of the following:

- grass for the children to play on

- a large paved area for outdoor entertainment
- a screened area for the clothesline, the compost, the rubbish and recycling bins, and the toolshed
- a couple of trees for climbing
- a small vegetable garden
- all-weather paths to the main doors
- privacy from neighbours
- a lemon tree
- a small swimming pool.

draw a plan

Measure your house and land, then draw the outline of the building on its site to a scale of 1:100 (1 cm equivalent to 1 m). Mark the direction of west as well as north so that you can see at a glance the hottest parts of the garden.

Indicate the windows and doors of the house: your requirements for shade, views and access are important. Make several photocopies of this site plan before you add anything else.

Professional garden designers sometimes use Melinex sheets (available from office suppliers) or tracing paper as overlays for trying out the shapes and patterns of items such as paths, terraces, pools, plants and pergolas. Formal and classical designs tend to be made up of squares and oblongs, informal and romantic ones of more loosely related curves.

You may prefer to work in pencil on a copy of the plan rather than on overlays, rubbing out and redrawing until you have something that is appealing, at least on paper.

Don't forget that your 'needs' must be considered at the same time as your 'likes', and that the position of the vegetable garden – not too close to moisture-robbing trees, and in full sun – may dictate the placing of several other elements. Even a very small swimming pool is such a dominating part of the average-size suburban garden that it will probably have to be the focal point.

Carry your best-looking plan around the space itself and try to visualise all those shapes three-dimensionally and in their wider context. You are sure to have to go on rubbing out and drawing again, but you will gradually feel more confident.

what about the plants?

Key plants, such as the climbable trees that some families would regard as essential, will be among the shapes drawn on the plan.

Choose other plants for any appropriate reason, including the following:

• because you are fond of them

- because they give your garden the kind of atmosphere you enjoy most (tropical rainforest, cottagey, Australian, European, Asian)
- because you know that their leaves, shapes or colours (all three if possible) sit well together
- for low maintenance
- for water-efficiency
- for their seasonal variations (shady in summer, colourful in autumn, bare in winter, covered with flowers in spring)
- to provide flowers, berries and foliage for all-year-round indoor decoration.

cool & temperate zones

Visit lots of gardens and broaden your ideas on design. Australia's Open Garden Scheme now covers hundreds of interesting private gardens in several states, and they are open to the public on specific days spread through most of the year.

Use your camera at home to record the development of the newly designed garden from its commencement. Take some photographs each season from the same position, so that you can see the changes taking place. Sometimes these pictures will enable you to improve on the design, or to correct planting errors before it is too late or while plants are relatively easy to move.

flowers to plant

Seed
candytuft
larkspur*
love-in-the-mist*

Seedlings
alyssum
candytuft
cineraria
forget-me-not
lupin
stock

vegetables to plant

Seed
bean, broad*
beetroot*
cabbage
capsicum
lettuce*
onion (late)

Seedlings
cabbage
cauliflower
leek
onion (midseason
and late)
spinach

COOL & TEMPERATE ZONES

vegetables . . . seed
pea*
silver beet
tomato

*Seed of these plants is best sown straight into the garden. Others should be sown in containers for transplanting later, or may be available now as seedlings.

other jobs for july

- Shift roses and other deciduous plants if necessary.
- Give bearded iris a dusting with bone meal and water it in around plants. Weed near all emerging bulbs and water in a pinch of complete fertiliser.
- Lift dahlia tubers and store them in sawdust to prevent drying out and rot.
- Apply liquid fertiliser to flower and vegetable seedlings.
- Plant two-year-old asparagus crowns 20 cm deep and 40 cm apart in rich soil (rotted animal manure, compost, and a handful of complete fertiliser per crown).
- Sow a 'green manure' crop (lupin, vetch, broad bean) in a vacant bed to add nitrogen and humus to the soil. Dig in just before it flowers, and plant vegetables six weeks later.

- Break up clumps of chives and shallots and replant plump offsets.
- Sprinkle and water in a small handful of complete fertiliser around herbs such as oregano, marjoram, sage and lemon balm. Dissolve a tablespoonful of sulphate of ammonia in half a watering-can of water and sprinkle it around parsley plants.
- Prune established hydrangeas to two-thirds their size, leaving about ten canes. Cut just above a pair of buds.
- Prune fuchsias to two-thirds their size, cutting just above a bud.
- Split up clumps of day lily (*Hemerocallis* species) after six or seven years, or if new plants are wanted.
- Plant rhubarb crowns in soil enriched with old manure, super-phosphate, and blood and bone. Give established plants a mulch of manure and a dressing of blood and bone.
- Spray deciduous fruit trees with dormant oil near end of month.

rose pruning

The easiest kinds of rose to prune are the 'old-fashioned' ones: you only need to remove unsightly and dead branches in winter.

Climbing species roses like the banksia rose can be pruned after they flower in spring if they are getting out of hand. Modern hybrid climbers usually need a light winter pruning.

Modern bush and standard roses are pruned fairly hard each July, although in very cold areas you should do the work in August.

By midwinter modern bush roses are straggly and have lost many of their leaves. They need fairly heavy pruning to get rid of dead wood and excess twigs, allowing room for vigorous new growth in spring. Prune as follows.

- Decide which four or five main stems to retain: a couple of them should, if possible, be strong green water shoots from just above the bulge of the budding union. Your aim should be to open up the centre of the plant, choosing a few healthy side shoots.
- Using sharp secateurs, cut back green stems to three or four buds, the top one preferably outward-pointing and with an angled 1 cm stub above it.
- Cut suckers to the ground (shoots from *below* the bulge made by the budding union).
- Rake up all prunings and destroy them, because they will be prickly and may be diseased.

looking good down south

- Iceland poppies in red, orange, yellow and white; the mauve *Iris unguicularis* peeping through foliage; early daffodils
- The silver–grey Cootamundra wattle (*Acacia baileyana*), with masses of yellow flowers

- The choice shrub *Luculia gratissima*: fragrant clusters of pink flowers against bronze leaves
- Fruiting and ornamental almonds, with white or pink blossom

subtropical & tropical zones

Turn your thoughts to garden design if you can spare the time between all the sowing of flower and vegetable seed and the planting of seedlings that can go on this month. Even a long-established garden benefits from a facelift, and July is an excellent month in the north for both planning and construction.

flowers to plant

Seed	*Seedlings*
ageratum	ageratum
alyssum	alyssum
aster	dianthus
candytuft	lupin

SUBTROPICAL & TROPICAL ZONES

flowers . . . seed	*flowers . . . seedlings*
cineraria	pansy
cosmos	petunia
dianthus	polyanthus
impatiens	portulaca
lupin	salvia
petunia	stock
phlox*	sunflower
portulaca	verbena
salvia	viola
verbena	viscaria*

vegetables to plant

Seed	*Seedlings*
bean, French*	broccoli
beetroot*	cabbage
broccoli	leek
cabbage	onion (midseason)
capsicum	silver beet
carrot*	spinach
cucumber*	tomato

vegetables . . . seed
lettuce*
marrow*
melon*
onion (late)
pea*
pumpkin*
radish*
silver beet
spinach
sweetcorn*
tomato
zucchini*

*Seed of these plants is best sown straight into the garden. Others should be sown in containers for transplanting later, or may be available now as seedlings.

other jobs for july

- Plant tropical bulbs such as hippeastrum, red nerine (*Nerine sarniensis*) and Amazon lily (*Eucharis grandiflora*).
- Plant offshoots of crucifix orchid (*Epidendrum* species) in pots or ordinary garden soil (provided that it is not heavy and wet).

SUBTROPICAL & TROPICAL ZONES

- Prune roses *lightly*.
- Inspect citrus trees for prominent bulges in stems from citrus gall wasp attack; prune below bulges and burn prunings at once.
- Sprinkle and water in a small handful of complete fertiliser around herbs such as parsley, oregano, marjoram, sage and lemon balm.
- Reduce watering of house-plants, but watch out for dry spots in the garden and water deeply when necessary.
- Spray any deciduous fruit trees with dormant oil near end of month.
- Plant grapevines (locally recommended varieties only) in the least humid parts of northern zones.
- Plant potatoes, sweet potatoes and shallots in the vegetable garden.
- Strike some cuttings of mulberry trees.

looking good up north

- Cornflowers (blue, pink, raspberry), lobelias, sweet peas and Virginian stock
- Brilliant red pea flowers on the bare limbs of the Indian coral tree (*Erythrina indica*)
- Weeping paperbark (*Melaleuca leucadendra*), with large cream bottlebrush flowers

basic tools for the garden

You will need most of these tools:

- a wheelbarrow
- a medium-weight spade and a long-handled shovel (preferably with a rolled-over top to the blade of each)
- a fork
- a rake and a hoe
- secateurs, a pruning saw and hedge-clippers
- a weeding implement, preferably hooked
- a lawnmower if you have lawn.

Garden tools will serve you best if you look after them.

- Store them together in a dry place.
- Sandpaper wooden handles occasionally and rub in raw linseed oil.
- Grease metal axles of wheelbarrows.
- Keep cutting implements sharp.
- Get the mower serviced regularly.

SUBTROPICAL & TROPICAL ZONES

august

a month for planting vegetables

JOB FILE

- *Plant the last of the deciduous trees, shrubs (including roses) and climbers, and prepare planting holes for evergreens*
- *Remove early buds from spring flower seedlings to strengthen plants*
- *Sprinkle all seedlings (flowers and vegetables) with liquid fertiliser*
- *Plant groundcovers to quell weed growth*
- *Begin to prepare ground for lawn-sowing in September*
- *Plant bulbs for summer and autumn flowering*

August is a good month in every part of Australia for planting a vegetable garden. Even the smallest yard has room for a few of the more compact vegetables, but there are three essentials:

- sunshine for most of the day
- well-prepared and well-drained soil
- plenty of water.

Many vegetables can be grown in tubs if space is scarce, although this kind of gardening takes devotion because tubs dry out very quickly.

choosing the site

Vegetables don't grow well in shade. It is even recommended that rows should run north and south to maximise sunlight. Tall plants like sweetcorn and climbing beans must be placed where they will not cast too much shadow on other vegetables.

preparing the soil

Most soils need special attention at the start, as well as supplements between crops. Good friable loam is best, but both sandy and clayey soils can be adapted to suit vegetables.

- Treat sandy soil by constantly adding as much compost and rotted animal manure as possible, and by digging in finished crops unless the ground is required at once.
- Treat clayey soil with gypsum: rake two to three cups into each square metre, together with compost and animal manure (repeat every six months or so).

Soil fertility is also important. Vegetables have specific needs for nutrients, and these elements are applied at planting time and (especially in the form of liquid fertiliser) as the plants grow. Nitrogen, phosphorus and potassium are the main ones, but trace elements are sometimes necessary too (molybdenum for cauliflowers, for example).

A good way of putting extra nitrogen into the soil is to sow a 'green manure' crop of leguminous plants such as vetch, lupins, or ordinary peas or beans. Chop into the soil when the flowers are still in bud, and allow to rot away for a few weeks before you plant a green-leaf crop (such as lettuce) that needs lots of nitrogen.

soil pH

Many vegetables have definite likes and dislikes when it comes to the acidity or alkalinity of soil. A pH reading of 7 indicates that the soil is neutral. Acid soil gives a lower reading and alkaline soil a higher one. Test your soil with a pH kit (available at garden shops), and rake in a cup of dolomite or lime per square metre if the soil is very acid; add barrowloads of animal manure and leaf mould if it is too alkaline.

Vegetables that prefer slightly alkaline soil include:

- beans, broccoli, brussels sprouts, cabbage, lettuce and peas
- cucumbers, pumpkins, marrows, melons and zucchini
- carrots, onions and parsnips
- asparagus, beetroot and sweetcorn.

Vegetables that prefer slightly acid soil include:

- potatoes and sweet potatoes
- radishes
- tomatoes.

improving the drainage

While very badly drained soil may need underground pipes to carry off excess water, raising vegetable beds is usually sufficient to ward off problems.

You'll need paths between plots, and soil removed from paths can be thrown onto adjacent beds to build them up. Adding compost and manure will raise the levels too.

watering

Steadily growing vegetables need no watering in damp, cool weather. Once conditions begin to dry out, however, they will soon falter if not kept moist. Thick mulch tucked around vegetables will help them cope with hot weather and reduce the amount of watering needed. Water as often as you are allowed by the laws of your area.

what to grow

Most of the common vegetables can be grown in any part of Australia (given the three essential conditions), as our zonal lists indicate. They are best planted in the recommended seasons, of course.

crop rotation

Don't plant vegetables from the same family in the same bed in consecutive years. The following are the main family groups:

- tomatoes, potatoes, capsicums and eggplant
- cabbage, broccoli, brussels sprouts and cauliflowers
- peas and beans
- cucumbers, pumpkins, marrows, melons and zucchini.

A good sequence for crops in the one bed would be:

- legumes (peas and beans)
- crucifers (cabbage, broccoli, cauliflower, kale) and other greens
- root vegetables (carrots, beetroot, potatoes, radishes) and onions
- cucurbits (cucumbers, pumpkin, zucchini, gourds)
- odds and ends, including celery, sweetcorn and tomatoes.

cool & temperate zones

If frost occurs in your area well into spring, delay the sowing and planting of tender vegetables until the risk is slight.

Young beans, capsicums, eggplant, tomatoes, and all members of the pumpkin family can be killed by frost. The leaves of potatoes can be bitten right back (though the plants usually recover), and frost at flowering time usually reduces pea yields. Anyone with a greenhouse has the opportunity to keep seedlings safe without falling far behind the schedule for warmer parts.

flowers to plant

Seed
ageratum
alyssum
aster
candytuft
larkspur*
lobelia*
phlox*

Seedlings
alyssum
candytuft
carnation
pansy
penstemon
petunia
polyanthus
primrose
portulaca
stock

vegetables to plant

Seed
beetroot*
capsicum

Seedlings
cabbage
capsicum

COOL & TEMPERATE ZONES

vegetables . . . seed
carrot*
cucumber*
eggplant
lettuce*
marrow*
parsnip*
pea*
pumpkin*
radish*
spinach
sweetcorn*
tomato

vegetables . . . seedlings
eggplant
onion (late)
silver beet
spinach

*Seed of these plants is best sown straight into the garden. Others should be sown in containers for transplanting later, or may be available now as seedlings.

other jobs for august

- Deadhead daffodils and other bulbs as they finish flowering.
- Sow seed and plant seedlings of any herb except basil (wait until days are really warm for that).

- Deadhead camellias and azaleas. Fertilise as soon as they finish flowering.
- Prune any untidy geraniums. Water in a handful of complete fertiliser around each.
- Dig flatweeds (root and all) out of lawns with an old knife, or spray with a selective herbicide.
- Sow a packet of mixed lettuce seed in the vegetable garden for interesting and colourful salads.
- Apply blueing compound to pink hydrangeas for a colour change.
- Plant potatoes in the vegetable garden.
- Spray with zineb any flowers showing signs of rust.
- Fertilise roses with animal manure (preferably cow manure) plus a handful of superphosphate, or with special rose food.
- Plant gladiolus corms for early flowers.
- Finish off winter pruning jobs.

cottage garden favourites

The idea of a romantic cottage garden, fragrant, flowery and informal, appeals to many people who don't live in cottages. A cottagey corner, at least, is possible in the garden around almost any kind of house. Here are some of the plants you might include in southern states:

COOL & TEMPERATE ZONES

- climbers such as jasmine, honeysuckle, and richly perfumed old-fashioned roses
- tall self-sowers such as foxgloves and hollyhocks
- tall perennials such as delphiniums and lupins
- medium perennials that also self-sow, such as valerian, lychnis (white or magenta) and columbine (aquilegia or granny's bonnet)
- self-sowing annuals such as love-in-the-mist, forget-me-nots and Shirley poppies
- low perennials such as violets, sea campion and perennial wallflowers
- herbs such as borage, thyme, marjoram, sage, curry plant
- daisies such as brachyscomes, shasta daisies, marguerites and Easter daisies
- several kinds of lavender, white or mauve.

looking good down south
- Broccoli and cauliflowers in abundance
- Freesias, hyacinths and daffodils at their height
- Wine-tinted or pink magnolias on leafless trees; camellias in many shades; white or pinkish wax-flowers
- Pussy willow (*Salix discolor*) with velvety grey buds

subtropical & tropical zones

Take advantage of the wide range of vegetables that can be grown in northern parts throughout the year, but try to maintain soil fertility at the same time. Compost everything that will rot down in your bin or heap, and beg or buy all the animal manure possible.

Since soils along the Queensland coast tend to be acid you will need to add lime, or preferably dolomite (which contains the extra element magnesium), for most vegetables. Further inland this may not be necessary.

Summer mulches in the north not only help to keep plants moist, but can also prevent compaction of the soil by pounding rains.

flowers to plant

Seed

ageratum

amaranthus*

aster

celosia

Seedlings

ageratum

alyssum

coleus

cosmos

SUBTROPICAL & TROPICAL ZONES

flowers . . . seed
coleus
cosmos
dianthus
lupin
petunia
phlox*
portulaca
salvia
zinnia

flowers . . . seedlings
dianthus
lupin
petunia
portulaca
salvia
verbena

vegetables to plant

Seed
bean, French*
beetroot*
broccoli
cabbage
capsicum
carrot*
cucumber*
lettuce*
marrow*

Seedlings
broccoli
cabbage
leek
onion (late)
silver beet
spinach
tomato

vegetables . . . seed
melon*
pumpkin*
radish*
silver beet
sweetcorn*
tomato
zucchini*

*Seed of these plants is best sown straight into the garden. Others should be sown in containers for transplanting later, or may be available now as seedlings.

other jobs for august

- Plant papaw seedlings as soon as the weather is warm.
- Prune bougainvilleas after flowering. Water and mulch well.
- Keep spring-flowering annuals weeded, and watered if necessary.
- Divide and replant any overcrowded bulbs such as tuberose, sprekelia and vallota.
- Try growing some colourful gourds for indoor decoration.
- Prune *Allamanda cathartica* (golden trumpet) heavily.
- Shift large shrubs if necessary.
- Plant potatoes and sweet potatoes. Mound soil around potatoes already growing.

SUBTROPICAL & TROPICAL ZONES

- Build a rock garden and prepare soil for planting.
- Dig over beds for dahlia planting in the next three months.
- Prune any untidy geraniums and apply a complete fertiliser.
- Divide and replant perennials such as gaillardia, gazania, rudbeckia and statice.
- Dig paspalum out of lawns if possible, or spray with a selective herbicide.
- Plant rhubarb crowns if you did not plant them in June.
- Spray with zineb any flowers showing signs of rust.
- Check orchid leaves for black mould. Carefully wipe affected leaves with household bleach diluted one part to four parts of water, washing it off a few minutes later (avoid splashing flowers).
- Plant more gladiolus corms.
- Sow seed (1.5 cm deep) of the Illawarra flame tree (*Brachychiton acerifolius*) in big pots, for planting out of seedlings next autumn.
- Take cuttings of acalypha, hibiscus and mussaenda.

looking good up north

- The scrambling Carolina jessamine (*Gelsemium sempervirens*), with sweet-scented yellow flowers
- The orchid-like yellow and brown flowers of the tamarind tree (*Tamarindus indica*)

- The chalice vine (*Solandra maxima*), with huge cup-shaped cream flowers

cleaning up the paths

Paths of gravel and wood shavings will need attention as weeds take off in the warmer weather. You can hand-weed between seasons, but herbicides may be necessary in spring and autumn, and it's then that they are most effective. Provided sprays can't leach into garden beds, paths are best treated with residual herbicides (rather than the non-residual glyphosate sprays) because they discourage new weeds. Use all herbicides sensibly and as infrequently as possible.

- Cover yourself up, and wear rubber gloves.
- Choose a calm, dry day (preferably *after* rain).
- Lock up pets, and keep young children indoors, until the spray has dried.
- To use the least possible herbicide, add marker dye to the mixture (ask at your garden shop) to show you where you've sprayed.
- Prevent drift by using a low-pressure sprayer or a watering-can with spraying bar attached.
- Do not spray any garden plants; cover those near paths with newspaper.
- Wash all equipment thoroughly after use.

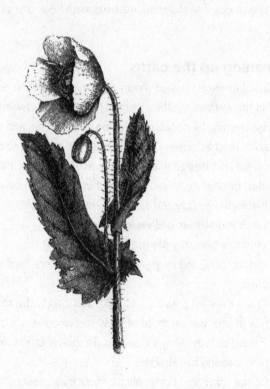

september

a month for catching spring

JOB FILE

- *Plant evergreen trees, shrubs and climbers, except for frost-tender ones in cold districts*
- *Plant new lawns everywhere, and fertilise established ones*
- *Tip-prune young native shrubs as they grow*
- *Spray weedy paths and patios with residual herbicides*
- *Spray areas required for new planting with non-residual, glyphosate-based herbicides – or redouble your weeding*
- *Plant any flower and vegetable seedlings from June container sowings*
- *Sow flower and vegetable seeds for summer planting*
- *Lay snailbait after rain*

To a gardener, catching spring means both enjoying the season and meeting its demands. If you have not kept up with your weeding and general maintenance in the garden, bulbs will be thrusting their way through choking mats instead of clean soil. If groundcovers were not cared for during winter, they will be struggling to do their weed-suppressing job now.

the pleasures of spring

Visit garden shows, nurseries, and private gardens offering open days. Make lists of the plants you like most, and notes on brilliant combinations to try. Watch out for the following spring-flowering plants, popular in most parts of Australia. The eucalypts mentioned, and species including *Ceanothus*, *Choisya*, *Campanula* (bellflowers) and *Felicia* (daisies), are not usually grown on the subtropical or tropical coasts.

Trees:

- ornamental fruit trees (mostly with pink or white blossoms) such as cherries, crab-apples, peaches and plums
- eucalypts such as *Eucalyptus caesia* (large, deep pink flowers) and *E. sideroxylon* (especially the form with flowers of a delicate pink)
- large wattles such as *Acacia cultriformis* (ball-shaped yellow flowers, dramatic triangular leaf-like phyllodes) and *A. floribunda* (yellow, rod-shaped flowers, graceful form and foliage).

Shrubs:

- the tropical *Calliandra* species, with pinkish-red tassel flowers
- the spring-flowering camellias, with pink, red or white flowers
- *Ceanothus* species and cultivars, with blue flowers
- *Choisya ternata* (Mexican orange blossom), with sweetly scented white flowers

- grevilleas, with red, apricot, cream, pink or magenta flowers
- lilacs, with white, pink, lilac or reddish purple flowers
- midseason rhododendrons, with flowers white to carmine.

Climbers:

- *Clematis aristatea*, with star-like cream flowers, tangled stems, tiny leaves
- *Cobaea scandens*, with cup-and-saucer flowers, green merging into purple
- *Hardenbergia comptoniana* (native wisteria), with purplish-blue pea flowers
- *Jasminum polyanthum* (jasmine), with fragrant white flowers
- *Pandorea pandorana* (wonga vine), with masses of tubular flowers – white, pink, brownish or purplish.

Groundcovers:

- *Ajuga reptans* (bugleweed), spreading perennial with purple flowers in spikes
- *Campanula poscharskyana*, spreading perennial with little bell-shaped mauve flowers
- *Dampiera linearis*, suckering native with yellow-centred blue flowers
- *Erigeron karvinskianus* (seaside daisy), self-sowing perennial with pink to white daisy flowers

- *Felicia amelloides* (blue marguerite), sprawling low-grower with blue or white daisy flowers.

Bulbs in flower, especially in the southern states:

- anemones
- bluebells
- daffodils
- Dutch iris
- freesias
- ranunculus
- sparaxis.

the demands of spring

You will enjoy your spring garden most if you have it under control. Keep down those intruder weeds as much as possible.

- Hand-weed or hoe to allow chosen plants the fertiliser and moisture intended for them. Do not let weeds go to seed and multiply your problems later. Put all annual weeds (but not perennial weeds like couch grass) straight into the compost bin or heap.
- Herbicides are best applied when weed growth is at its most vigorous. Use quick-acting but non-residual herbicides if you plan to replant an area. Residual herbicides will kill off all growth for

some months; use them only on paths and between the pavers or bricks in patios and courtyards (see 'Cleaning up the paths' on page 125).

Make use of your pruning gear:

- Deadhead annuals and perennials as they fade, to encourage further flowering.
- Tip-prune new growth on native shrubs to keep them busy.
- Tidy shrubs with secateurs or hedge-clippers as they finish blooming. Cut back new growth by at least a third on rangy shrubs like buddleja, forsythia, philadelphus and japonica. Very old wood can be sawn off at ground level.
- Prune bottlebrushes (*Callistemon* species and cultivars) just below the flowerheads as soon as they start to turn brown.

Watch out for damaging pests:

- Aphids often spoil flowers at bud stage. Rub or hose them off whenever you see them. Spray extensive infestations with a pyrethrum-based insecticide.
- Slugs and snails relish young plants and damp conditions. Lay snailbait in tiny heaps (choose the animal-friendly variety, in case birds, cats or dogs eat it).
- European mites and two-spotted mites are hard to see, but turn green leaves pale and mottled. Spraying with a miticide containing

dicofol helps, but it's best to avoid such chemicals. Organic oils and sprays are available.

Maintain the fertilising:

- Sprinkle liquid fertiliser fortnightly on quick-growing plants such as vegetables and annual flowers.
- Spread complete fertiliser or blood and bone under the outer leaves of shrubs, climbers and young ornamental trees and water it in (fork holes help penetration).
- Mulch plants with home-made or mushroom compost.

Compare your garden with others you see:

- Is there a good balance of flower and foliage?
- Do any plants clash in colour, texture, character or proportion?
- Are there gaps to be filled?
- Are some plants becoming crowded?
- Is there somewhere pleasant to sit?

cool & temperate zones

Visiting nurseries to see what's looking good is one thing; buying the right plants is another. Few nursery labels tell you enough to avoid expensive errors. The lovely weeping *Eucalyptus caesia*, for example, is 'small' but it usually grows to at least 6 m tall and 2.5 m wide. Those grevilleas may tempt you, but they won't thrive in solid shade, so buy them only if you have sunny patches to offer.

flowers to plant

Seed	*Seedlings*
ageratum	ageratum
alyssum	alyssum
aster	aster
candytuft	candytuft
cosmos	carnation
hollyhock*	delphinium
larkspur*	petunia
linaria*	portulaca

flowers . . . seed
lobelia*
love-in-the-mist*
lupin
mignonette*
nasturtium*
nemesia*

vegetables to plant

Seed
beetroot*
cabbage
capsicum
carrot*
celery
cucumber*
eggplant
lettuce*
marrow*
parsnip*
pea*

Seedlings
cabbage
capsicum
onion (late)
silver beet
tomato

COOL & TEMPERATE ZONES

vegetables . . . seed
pumpkin*
radish*
silver beet
spinach
sweetcorn*
tomato
zucchini*

*Seed of these plants is best sown straight into the garden. Others should be sown in containers for transplanting later, or may be available now as seedlings.

other jobs for september

- Examine your eucalypts for caterpillars: squirming black clusters of 'spitfires', or leaf-covering hairy skeletonisers. Snip off branchlets or leaves and squash caterpillars.
- Spray flowering strawberries with benomyl against botrytis mould (repeat in two weeks).
- Dust sulphate of ammonia along rows of emerging potato plants (repeat in three weeks), and plant more (try a different variety).
- Check lawns: topdress low areas with sand and re-sow bare patches.

- Fertilise fruit trees again, as you did in April.
- Spray deciduous fruit trees with Bordeaux mixture or copper oxychloride as buds swell, then with benomyl when in early bloom.
- Deadhead spring bulbs as they finish, but do not cut stems or leaves until they dry off.
- Plant gladiolus corms.
- Attend to house-plants – cut off dry or unsightly twigs and leaves, fertilise, and re-pot if necessary.
- Choose healthy outer suckers from chrysanthemums to replant.
- Postpone pruning of shrubs such as fuchsia, hibiscus, jacobinia and luculia if there is any chance of late frosts.

looking good down south

- Tulips, bluebells and Dutch iris
- Twining sarsaparilla (*Hardenbergia violacea*), smothered in purple, pink or white pea flowers
- The early crab-apple *Malus spectabilis* 'Plena', with double pink flowers; fruiting quinces, with their single blooms of palest pink

to stake or not to stake?

Tall-growing perennials (dahlias, Easter dishes, delphiniums, for example) and annuals (sunflowers, for example) generally need to be staked.

COOL & TEMPERATE ZONES

- Use stakes that are as inconspicuous as possible, and hide them among foliage if you can.
- Stake tuberous plants like dahlias at planting time (to avoid skewering tubers later), and other kinds when they are in bud.
- Use only enough stakes to support the plant.
- Tie with soft material such as lengths of pantyhose leg.

Staking trees and shrubs is often avoidable if you choose small, sturdy plants that will anchor themselves as they grow; spindly ones can be cut back.

- If staking is essential, use two or three stakes and tie with pantyhose or binder twine.
- Remove stakes as soon as plants are stable.

subtropical & tropical zones

Areas inland may still be having the occasional frost but in most parts of the north it is noticeably warming up. Plant trees, shrubs, and flower and vegetable seedlings now so that they are moving well before the weather gets really hot. Don't forget to keep up the watering until nature takes over the job.

SUBTROPICAL & TROPICAL ZONES

flowers to plant

Seed	*Seedlings*
ageratum	ageratum
amaranthus*	alyssum
aster	aster
celosia	celosia
coleus	coleus
cosmos	cosmos
dianthus	dianthus
petunia	lupin
phlox*	petunia
portulaca	portulaca
salvia	salvia
torenia	verbena
zinnia	zinnia

vegetables to plant

Seed	*Seedlings*
bean, French*	broccoli
beetroot*	cabbage
cabbage	capsicum

vegetables . . . seed

capsicum

carrot*

cucumber*

eggplant

lettuce*

marrow*

melon*

pumpkin*

radish*

silver beet

sweetcorn*

zucchini*

vegetables . . . seedlings

onion (late)

silver beet

spinach

tomato

*Seed of these plants is best sown straight into the garden. Others should be sown in containers for transplanting later, or may be available now as seedlings.

other jobs for september

- Prune hibiscus so that they quickly make new growth and flower again in a couple of months.
- Plant tubers of the splendid foliage plant caladium in a protected, shady spot.

- Plant some herbs in pots, for easy moving when heavy rains come.
- Complete preparation of ground for new lawns (see page xx). Use a complete fertiliser high in nitrogen on existing lawns.
- Plant potatoes and sweet potatoes. Dust sulphate of ammonia along rows of emerging potato plants (repeat in three weeks).
- Plant shooting dahlia tubers for early blooms.
- Fertilise fruit trees again, as you did in April.
- Plant an indigenous Queensland tree such as *Buckinghamia celsissima* (ivory curl), *Callistemon viminalis* (weeping bottlebrush), *Grevillea hillii* or *G. robusta* (silky oak).
- Spray deciduous fruit trees with Bordeaux mixture or copper oxychloride as buds swell, then with benomyl when in early bloom.
- Plant rock gardens; choose low, mounding but not rampant plants interspersed with taller-growing species.
- Re-pot indoor plants in fresh potting mix. Prune roots to fit or move to a pot one size larger. Mulch well.
- Plant bromeliad suckers in shady places.
- Take cuttings of poinsettia.
- Choose some groundcovers for bare patches – ajuga, plectranthus, balsam (*Impatiens* species).
- Put up some hanging baskets in shady places, and water them daily.
- Plant avocadoes, custard apples, lychees, macadamias, mangoes,

SUBTROPICAL & TROPICAL ZONES

mulberry trees, sapodillas and star fruits; try rambutans if you live north of Cairns.

looking good up north

- Bird of paradise (*Strelitzia reginae*), with large, striking orange and blue flowers on tall stems
- Star of jasmine (*Trachelospermum jasminoides*), with sweet-smelling starry white flowers
- The delicate mauve flowers of the white cedar (*Melia azedarach* var. *australasica*)

plant a choko

This perennial vegetable is related to melons and zucchini but is best grown over a fence or substantial trellis rather than on the ground. It thrives in frost-free northern regions, where it will fruit at least twice a year. Now is the time to plant chokos.

- Prepare a wide, deep hole in a well-drained position, enriching the soil with compost and animal manure plus about a cup of complete fertiliser.
- Buy or beg a whole fruit and wait until it sends up a shoot.
- Bury the fruit just below the soil on an angle and with the shoot pointing downwards.

- Water well, and continue to water in dry weather. The vine will grow rapidly.
- Pick and eat the fruit while it is young and tender.
- Once a plant is established it should receive about a cup of complete fertiliser every spring.

SUBTROPICAL & TROPICAL ZONES

october

a month for thinking Australian

JOB FILE

- *Plant some Australian species*
- *Encourage birds into the garden*
- *Attend native plant shows in your area*
- *Deadhead spring annuals and feed with liquid fertiliser for further blooming*
- *Sow flower and vegetable seed for autumn planting*
- *Plant flower and vegetable seedlings from July and August container sowings*
- *Plant or prune frost-tender trees (including citrus), shrubs and climbers if danger of frost is over*

Many Australian gardens contain no Australian plants at all. Few gardens are solely devoted to them. Isn't it time to swing the balance the other way?

October is a month when a large number of natives are flowering. Nurseries are full of attractive plants looking for a home, and staff members are generally well informed about them. Most of the Australian plants now available have been cultivated by enthusiasts for years. Those found unsuitable for gardens have dropped out of the market, and you are not likely to be sold impossibly difficult species. Detailed information is now available in numerous books and magazine articles devoted to indigenous Australian plants.

choosing plants

Good nurseries stock trees, shrubs, climbers, groundcovers and rockery plants that broadly suit local climate and soil, but it's always best to do your homework before buying.

- Climate is not always relevant. Many Australian plants do well in places climatically very different from their original home. You can plant a shrub that likes warmth in a sunny, sheltered position, for instance, but there is not much point in choosing frost-tender plants if you have frequent frosts, or plants that cannot stand humidity if you live on the subtropical or tropical coast.
- Soil can be adapted to some extent. Heavy clays can be lightened with applications of gypsum and compost, and a mound of sand will allow you to grow some of the Western Australian species that might otherwise be impossible. Good drainage is necessary, in fact, for all but the swamp-lovers.

placing plants

Bear in mind the following when deciding where to put your indigenous plants:

- their ability to blend with plants already in the garden

- potential height and width
- preference for moisture or dryness, sun or shade
- suitability for pots, tubs or hanging baskets
- capacity to attract birds
- any tendency to block drains.

combining australian plants and exotics

Exotics and natives can look good in the one garden, but there are things to avoid:

- clashes of character – informal-looking natives like eucalypts do not usually sit well alongside formal exotic plants like conifers
- clashes in foliage – the weeping leaves of some wattles look odd near the large, shiny leaves of camellias
- clashes in flower colour – plan colour combinations carefully.

Australian plants and exotics should not always be treated the same way. Watch out for the following:

- soil preferences – positions suitable for exotics may not be well enough drained for some natives
- fertiliser problems – over-fertilising can harm many natives, and banksias, grevilleas and hakeas are particularly sensitive to phosphorus (found especially in superphosphate and complete fertilisers); slow-release fertilisers and blood and bone are safer

- watering – Australian plants may require less water than exotics.
In a mixed garden, grouping natives with natives and exotics with
exotics solves many visual and practical problems.

some popular australian plants for small gardens

The following small trees and significant shrubs particularly suit the
areas they are listed under, but will all grow elsewhere.

For cool areas:

- *Acacia boormanii* (Snowy River wattle), medium to large shrub with
grey foliage and yellow flowers in winter
- *Eucalyptus pauciflora* (snow gum), small to medium tree with
interesting bark and white flowers from spring to summer
- *Eucryphia lucida* (leatherwood), medium tree with glossy leaves
and white (or pale pink) flowers in summer
- *Telopea truncata* (Tasmanian waratah), medium shrub with scarlet
flowers in summer.

For temperate areas:

- *Acmena smithii* (lilly pilly), medium tree with attractive globular
fruit (white, pinkish or purple) in winter
- *Banksia spinulosa* (giant candles or haipin banksia), small to
medium shrub with orange and black flowers from autumn to
winter

- *Eucalyptus leucoxylon* subspecies *megalocarpa*, a medium tree variable in form and flower colour (often deep pink) and blooming at almost any time of year
- *Hakea laurina* (pincushion hakea), large shrub with globular deep-pink flowers in autumn.

For warm and subtropical areas:

- *Acacia podalyriifolia* (Mount Morgan or Queensland silver wattle), medium tree with silver foliage and large golden flowers in winter and spring
- *Backhousia citriodora* (lemon-scented myrtle), medium tree with fragrant leaves and creamish flowers from summer to autumn
- *Melaleuca styphelioides* (prickly paperbark), medium tree with peeling papery bark and small white bottlebrushes in summer
- *Persoonia pinifolia* (pine-leaf geebung), tall shrub with weeping habit and golden flowerheads from summer to autumn.

cool & temperate zones

Visit the public wildflower gardens in your locality, for example Kings Park in Perth, Wittunga in the Adelaide Hills, the Maranoa Gardens in Melbourne, Canberra's Australian National Botanic Gardens, or the Ku-ring-gai Wildflower Garden in Sydney.

The Society for Growing Australian Plants (contact the regional society in your state or Territory) is well worth joining. Membership fees are low, and you can receive the botanical journal *Australian Plants* in addition to the branch newsletters, which are full of helpful hints. You can also learn a lot at meetings, and have free access to the seed bank of the Society for Growing Australian Plants with its hundreds of species.

flowers to plant

Seed
ageratum
alyssum
aster

Seedlings
ageratum
alyssum
aster

COOL & TEMPERATE ZONES

flowers . . . seed
cosmos
hollyhock*
larkspur*
linaria*
lobelia*
love-in-the-mist*
lupin
mignonette*
nasturtium*
petunia
phlox*
portulaca
salvia
Virginian stock*
viscaria*
zinnia

flowers . . . seedlings
candytuft
carnation
petunia
portulaca
verbena
zinnia

vegetables to plant

Seed
bean, French*
beetroot*

Seedlings
cabbage
capsicum

vegetables . . . seed
broccoli
cabbage
capsicum
carrot*
cauliflower
celery
cucumber*
eggplant
lettuce*
marrow*
melon*
parsnip*
pea*
pumpkin*
radish*
silver beet
spinach
sweetcorn*
tomato
zucchini*

vegetables . . . seedlings
cauliflower
celery
eggplant
leek
tomato

COOL & TEMPERATE ZONES

*Seed of these plants is best sown straight into the garden. Others should be sown in containers for transplanting later, or may be available now as seedlings.

other jobs for october

- Photograph the garden.
- Scrub off patches of scale, or spray affected plants with white oil.
- Plant gladiolus corms.
- Look out for early aphids on roses. Rub them off with your fingers, or use a tissue soaked in a solution of household detergent.
- Mow lawns regularly and water well when necessary.
- Dust sulphate of ammonia along rows of flowering potato plants and water it in; mound soil around them.
- Sow seed and plant seedlings of all herbs, including basil.
- Spray stone fruits with benomyl when they are in early bloom.
- As soon as they have finished flowering, prune boronia, callistemon, ceanothus, ceratostigma, choisya, diosma, felicia, forsythia, mintbush, ornamental peach and plum, philadelphus, protea, spiraea, wattle and wax-flower.
- Spray apple and pear trees with maldison when most of the petals have fallen, then every three weeks until harvest with carbaryl.
- Plant evergreen trees, shrubs, climbers and groundcovers.
- Prepare rich soil for dahlia-planting next month.
- Plant passionfruit, and prune established vines by reducing trailing arms to about 60 cm with hedge-clippers.
- Take softwood and semi-hardwood cuttings to grow new plants.

- Finish fertilising fruit trees.
- Apply liquid fertiliser fortnightly to flowers and vegetables.

looking good down south

- Columbines, cornflowers, love-in-the-mist, nasturtiums, Shirley poppies, violas
- Two shrubs: the fountain buddleja (*Buddleja alternifolia*), with arching trusses of sweet-smelling mauve flowers; philadelphus, with fragrant white blooms
- Wisteria, mauve or white, draped over pergolas and verandahs; the climbing banksia rose, yellow or white
- The Flinders Range wattle (*Acacia iteaphylla*), its pods a conspicuous silver; pinoaks in delicate new leaf

bringing in the birds

Birds make any garden more interesting. Australian plants particularly attract native birds, but the berries on exotic shrubs such as hawthorns and pyracanthas are relished by crimson and eastern rosellas, gang-gang cockatoos and other parrots.

Here are some tips for bringing birds into your garden.

- Give them plenty of places to perch and hide. Have a mixture of trees and shrubs; tangled shrubs like correas and prickly ones like

COOL & TEMPERATE ZONES

some hakeas suit little birds, including scrubwrens and spinebills.

- Choose plants that supply food (nectar, seeds and insects) for birds. Grevilleas are among the best.
- Discourage or confine cats if possible.
- Make water available. Suspended water bowls are safest for birds, but you must keep them filled.

subtropical & tropical zones

Northern gardeners are better placed than most to create an Australian rainforest garden. There is a wonderful range of native palms, creepers, ferns and orchids available, and small plants that particularly thrive in shade can be included. Be sure to plant at least one blueberry ash (*Elaeocarpus reticulatus*) in your little rainforest.

A mist-watering system, to be turned on in certain parts of the garden when the humidity becomes low, will not only keep the plants comfortable but encourage mosses to cover trunks and carpet the ground.

SUBTROPICAL & TROPICAL ZONES

flowers to plant

Seed

ageratum
amaranthus*
aster
celosia
coleus
cosmos
salvia
torenia
zinnia

Seedlings

ageratum
aster
celosia
coleus
cosmos
petunia
portulaca
salvia
zinnia

vegetables to plant

Seed

bean, French*
beetroot*
cabbage
capsicum
carrot*
cucumber*
eggplant

Seedlings

broccoli
cabbage
capsicum
silver beet
tomato

vegetables . . . seed
lettuce*
marrow*
melon*
pumpkin*
radish*
silver beet
sweetcorn*
zucchini*

*Seed of these plants is best sown straight into the garden. Others should be sown in containers for transplanting later, or may be available now as seedlings.

other jobs for october

- Increase mulches as weather becomes hotter.
- Plant sweet potatoes in the vegetable garden.
- Dust young cabbage plants, and others in the same family, with derris to deter cabbage moths and butterflies.
- Take softwood and semi-hardwood cuttings.
- Mow lawns regularly and water deeply when necessary.
- Water mangoes and lychees for good fruit development.

- Give house-plants a dose of slow-release fertiliser, and take some cuttings to pot up for Christmas.
- Wipe leaves of indoor palms with a cloth dipped in water plus a few drops of detergent.
- Finish fertilising fruit trees and plant all tropical fruits.
- Plant more dahlia tubers and summer-flowering bulbs.
- Do not allow citrus trees to dry out.
- Deadhead roses and give a side dressing of fertiliser. Rub or wash off any aphids.
- Apply liquid fertiliser to flowers and vegetables.
- Scrub off patches of scale, or spray affected plants with white oil.
- Divide and replant cannas.
- Try some frangipani cuttings – use branch-size pieces, rub them in dirt to stop them weeping, and leave to dry before inserting deeply in garden soil.
- Check gardenias for leaf yellowing due to magnesium deficiency; ask for a supplement at your nursery.
- Plant palms, but ensure good drainage.
- Plant tree ferns between now and December.
- Prune poinsettia for sturdier growth (but avoid its poisonous sap).
- Plant crotons to brighten dull corners, but make sure they get plenty of sun (take some cuttings for further plants).

SUBTROPICAL & TROPICAL ZONES

looking good up north

- Ageratum, alyssum, lupins, pansies, sunflowers
- Fragrant creamish flowers on the native frangipani (*Hymenosporum flavum*)
- The tree waratah (*Alloxylon flammeum*), with large reddish flowers

choice shrubs for northern gardens

These Australian shrubs grow well in subtropical and tropical areas.

- *Austromyrtus dulcis* (midgen berry)
  The midgen spreads wider than its height of 0.5–1.5 m. New growth is pink, and both the little white flowers (autumn to winter) and the brownish or mauve berries are attractive.
- *Callistemon* ('Reeves Pink')
  The large pink bottlebrush flowers of this 2–3 m shrub appear in late spring; cut off as many as possible as they fade.
- *Gardenia ochreata* (native gardenia)
  The leaves of this hard-to-get 2–5 m shrub may fall in dry seasons without harming it. Prune to keep it bushy. The large, fragrant white flowers bloom in spring.
- *Melaleuca bracteata* ('Golden Gem')
  This hardy melaleuca (green with gold tips) grows to about 2 m high and wide. Small white bottlebrushes appear in summer.

november

a month to build

JOB FILE

- *Start mulching seriously*
- *Plant trees, shrubs, climbers and groundcovers everywhere*
- *Liquid-fertilise vegetables*
- *Plant flower and vegetable seedlings from August and September container sowings*
- *Spray aphid-infested roses with pyrethrum*
- *Dig out a few potatoes*
- *Spray the leaves of fruit trees with pyrethrum or carbaryl if pear and cherry slugs are evident*

Elaborate construction projects in the garden are best left to professionals, but there are plenty of simple do-it-yourself jobs for home-owners to tackle. You'll save money, and perhaps even enjoy, trying your hand at one or more of the following.

Once you have developed your skills you may graduate to pergolas, barbecues, arches, brick-paved courtyards, gazebos, walled rose-gardens . . .

diy gravelling

Gravel drives and paths are much cheaper than ones paved with brick, stone or slate. Even concrete, in poured or slab form, costs quite a bit more than gravel, and except on a small scale is beyond the skills of many do-it-yourselfers in any case.

For medium to large areas gravel is attractive and easy to put down, though one limitation is its unsuitability for steeply sloping sites. It also needs regular raking and weed control.

Here's how to lay a gravel drive or path.

- Mark your boundaries with string attached to short pegs.
- Dig out the soil within the markers to a depth of about 15 cm in the centre and about 20 cm near the edges, that is, with a drainage hump along the middle.
- For a long driveway dig a couple of sloping trenches across the track to accommodate polythene drainpipe of an appropriate size. Slope your trenches towards whichever side of the driveway can best handle stormwater.
- Order enough coarse crushed rock to provide a foundation that will pack down to about 15 cm (the supplier will help you to estimate quantities). Choose and order, for delivery later, your more expensive topping material. Crushed limestone ('Lilydale toppings' in Victoria) includes fine particles that assist compaction, and you'll need a layer about 5 cm thick; if you choose screenings (gravel consisting of small water-washed pebbles), a shallower layer

(about 2.5 cm thick) will be advisable so that it does not roll or sink underfoot.

- Rake the crushed rock (maintaining the hump), and use a hired or borrowed roller or compacter to consolidate it thoroughly.
- Take delivery of your topping material, and rake, water and roll the final layer.

diy retaining walls

There are many gardens that need a retaining wall, usually to prevent a bank slipping onto a flat area. Amateurs should not attempt high retaining walls, which may have to be built from brick or stone and must be properly engineered.

Most people can, however, manage a 60 cm wall constructed inexpensively from old railway sleepers or equivalent slabs of new timber. The first step is to locate a supply of sleepers or slabs and check their size: the following instruction assume that they are about 22 cm wide, 12 cm deep and 2.7 m long, but yours may be different.

- Calculate and order the number of sleepers you need, allowing for groups of three, one on top of the other, plus a half-length to cover each junction vertically, and a couple of extras in case of accidents.
- Lay out your sleepers near the bank in well-matched trios,

trimming any ragged ends but keeping each trio the same length.

- Shear the excess soil and clay vertically from your bank at about the 60 cm level, and get it out of the way.
- Buy a supply of bolts (without nuts) about 1 cm diameter and 25 cm long, allowing two to each sleeper. You'll also need two shorter bolts (about 21 cm) for each of the junctions.
- Dig a trench about 6 cm deep and 12 cm wide along the base of the cut, and lower the first row of sleepers into it on their edges, with the neater 22 cm face outwards. Firm the soil around the base.
- Drill a hole, the same diameter as your bolts, about 5 cm from the top and end of each sleeper and tap the bolts deep into the bank.
- Align the second row of sleepers on top of the first, and similarly 'bolt' them to the bank.
- Drill the bolt hole for the third row of sleepers about 5 cm from the bottom, not the top, of each, and knock in the bolts as before. Don't forget about these bolts when you are digging later.
- Saw about 50 cm from each of your junction sleepers, then divide the remainder into two pieces, each about 110 cm long.
- Dig a hole at the bottom of each junction point, just big enough to insert a half-sleeper vertically, and deep enough (about 50 cm) that the top aligns with those of the horizontal sleepers.

- About 5 cm from the top and end of each pair of adjoining horizontal sleepers, drill a bolt hole from the *inside* (scrape back the soil if necessary). Get someone to maintain pressure on the front of the vertical sleeper while you drill about two-thirds of the way into it from the other side and tap the bolt through the horizontal sleeper and as far as possible into the vertical one.
- Tamp the soil firmly around the vertical sleepers and backfill the top row.

diy rockwork

Natural outcrops of attractive boulders in gardens are rare, but you can create a natural-looking outcrop if you are careful as well as strong.

- Plan the position for your outcrop and decide what to do about plants – keep them sparse, to highlight the rocks, or allow them to dominate the picture?
- Locate a supplier and choose your rocks – three to five may be enough. A mixture of sizes is essential and, particularly if you want the outcrop to make a reasonable impact, you should include a couple that take two people to lift.
- Dig up the soil to a depth of about 20 cm (more for large boulders) and use a stick to mark the ground with the approximate shape of

each rock. When you are satisfied with the arrangement of shapes, prepare to move the largest rocks into position.

- Remove enough soil for the rocks to be deeply embedded, and jiggle them into place. Keep fiddling with them until they look exactly right and cannot wobble.
- Add the smaller rocks, and check the appearance of the collection from every angle.
- Push good soil around all the rocks, and plant – according to your initial plan – as soon as you have recovered your breath.

cool & temperate zones

Choose a cool day for major DIY jobs. The increasing need for shade at this time of year may suggest some minor DIY handiwork as well. Shadecloth fixed over or under any pergolas that are not yet covered with creepers will help you and your hanging baskets to stay comfortable.

flowers to plant

Seed	*Seedlings*
aster	ageratum
cosmos	alyssum
linaria*	aster
lupin	candytuft
mignonette*	carnation
nasturtium*	cosmos
petunia	delphinium
phlox*	lupin
portulaca	petunia
salvia	portulaca
sweet william	salvia
verbena	verbena
viscaria*	zinnia

vegetables to plant

Seed	*Seedlings*
bean, French*	cabbage
beetroot*	capsicum
broccoli	celery

vegetables . . . seed	*vegetables . . . seedlings*
cabbage	eggplant
capsicum	leek
carrot*	silver beet
celery	spinach
cucumber*	tomato
lettuce*	
marrow*	
melon*	
onion, white*	
parsnip*	
pea*	
pumpkin*	
radish*	
silver beet	
spinach	
sweetcorn*	
tomato	
zucchini*	

COOL & TEMPERATE ZONES

*Seed of these plants is best sown straight into the garden. Others should be sown in containers for transplanting later, or may be available now as seedlings.

COOL & TEMPERATE ZONES

other jobs for november

- Lift tulip bulbs and store them in a dry place for autumn planting.
- Attend rose and rhododendron shows.
- Lift and divide polyanthus primrose and violets, and replant outer pieces.
- Look for pear and cherry slugs on leaves of hawthorns, plums, pears, cherries and quinces. Talcum powder works well on small areas. Alternatively, spray with pyrethrum or carbaryl.
- Plant potatoes in the vegetable garden.
- Keep green vegetables moving with fortnightly doses of liquid fertiliser.
- Try some interesting beans – golden butter beans, purple varieties (which turn green when cooked) or perennial climbers such as scarlet runner.
- Prune shrubs, if necessary, as they finish flowering.
- Take semi-hardwood cuttings of buddleja, camellia and grevillea, and tip cuttings of azalea.
- Plant dahlia tubers and gladiolus corms.
- Spray apple and pear trees every three weeks with carbaryl against codling moth and light brown apple moth.
- Submerge pots and hanging baskets in a bucket or trough of water and remove when bubbling stops.

- Prune male kiwi-fruit vines after flowers fade (flowers on male plants have a mass of stamens but no central white 'style').
- Scrub off patches of scale, or spray affected plants with white oil.
- Mulch shallow-rooted plants.

small plants for dry spots

Gardens even in the cooler parts of Australia have dry corners where only the toughest drought-resisters will thrive. Plants such as the following are ideal for arid regions too.

- *Crassula* species (crassula)
  Try the fairy crassula, a groundcover with tiny pale pink flowers on 30 cm stems.
- *Mesembryanthemum* species (pigface)
  The many-petalled, satiny flowers of these succulents open wide in the sun. Colours tend to be blindingly bright.
- *Pelargonium* species (pelargoniums and geraniums)
  Pelargoniums include the ivy-leaved climbers, the large-flowered geraniums, and many species with fragrant leaves (lemon, peppermint, rose and so on). Flower colours vary.
- *Sedum* species (stonecrop)
  There is a range of colours in the flower heads that rise from these low-growing, fleshy plants.

COOL & TEMPERATE ZONES

- *Sempervivum* species (houseleek)
  The succulent rosettes of leaves on the sempervivums are vaguely cabbagey; reddish flower heads appear in summer.

looking good down south

- Strawberry plants covered with flowers and fruit
- Kangaroo paws (red, green, yellow) and November lilies (white)
- Red, burgundy, pink and green bottlebrushes (*Callistemon* species and cultivars); pale-pink heads on the Persian lilac
- Honeysuckle and jasmine (smelling good too)
- *Virgilia capensis* (Cape virgilia), with fragrant mauve pea flowers

COOL & TEMPERATE ZONES

subtropical & tropical zones

The wet season will thoroughly test your DIY gravelling, retaining walls and rockwork. In areas of very high rainfall it may be necessary to use brick or stone in even a medium-height wall, with weepholes near the bottom to prevent a build-up of water behind it.

flowers to plant

Seed	*Seedlings*
ageratum	ageratum
amaranthus*	celosia
celosia	coleus
coleus	cosmos
salvia	petunia
torenia	portulaca
zinnia	salvia
	torenia
	zinnia

vegetables to plant

Seed	*Seedlings*
cabbage	cabbage
capsicum	capsicum
carrot*	eggplant
cucumber*	silver beet
eggplant	
lettuce*	
marrow*	
melon*	
pumpkin*	
radish*	
silver beet	
sweetcorn*	
zucchini*	

*Seed of these plants is best sown straight into the garden. Others should be sown in containers for transplanting later, or may be available now as seedlings.

other jobs for november

- Broadcast gypsum over lawns and water in well. Plant new lawns.
- Hang fruit fly baits in fruit trees and spray with fenthion.

- Plant a king orchid (*Dendrobium speciosum*) in a tree that offers dappled shade.
- Divide potted orchids and replant in orchid potting mix (but not if they are flowering).
- Keep green vegetables moving with fortnightly doses of liquid fertiliser.
- Plant sweet potatoes in the vegetable garden.
- Avoid overhead watering in high humidity, to reduce the incidence of fungal diseases.
- Check the garden for areas prone to erosion. Very thick mulching will help.
- Scrub off patches of scale, or spray affected plants with white oil – but not on a hot day.
- Check roses for diseased leaves, which should be removed and destroyed.
- Remove faded flowers from hippeastrums, but do not cut down stems until they have dried off.
- Plant dahlia tubers and gladiolus corms.
- Trim wattles for bushier, more robust plants.
- Plant bananas, using disease-free stock: observe local regulations.
- Fertilise established bananas every two months with a formulation rich in potash; water regularly.

SUBTROPICAL & TROPICAL ZONES

- Take cuttings of bougainvillea.
- Prune rambling roses if they are rambling too far.
- Check ripeness of watermelons by tapping: they are ready to pick if hollow-sounding.
- Pick ripe mulberries.
- Plant all the tropical fruit trees you are interested in establishing.
- Inspect trees for borer attack. If borer holes are found, try to skewer the insects with a thin wire, or consult a tree surgeon regarding valuable trees if the damage looks extensive.
- Hand-pollinate flowering pumpkins if fruit is not setting: dust pollen from male flowers (smaller) into the centre of female flowers.

looking good up north

- Day lilies (*Hemerocallis* species) in a range of soft colours – a new cluster each morning
- The brilliant blue fruits of the indigenous tree blue quandong (*Elaeocarpus angustifolia*)
- Moreton Bay chestnut (*Castanospermum australe*) with clusters of red–orange pea flowers

what's in a name?

Botanical names need not puzzle you, and they can be helpful. Here is an example that explains the plant-naming system used throughout the world:

- Family: Mimosaceae
- Genus: *Acacia*
- Species: *baileyana*
- Common name: Cootamundra wattle.

Note that Latin forms are used: *baileyana* is simply a latinised version of Bailey, the name of a botanist commemorated by the species. Often the species name describes a characteristic, for example *parviflora* means 'with small flowers'.

Acacia baileyana happens to be widely known by its common name, but some plants have none. Since there is a botanical name for every plant, it makes sense to use that if there is any chance of confusion. On the other hand you can refer to all members of the genus *Acacia* as acacias, and most people call *Lactuca sativa* a lettuce.

Cultivated varieties of plants (cultivars) have non-latinised 'fancy names' placed between single inverted commas. *Grevillea* 'Robyn Gordon' is one of the many grevillea cultivars.

december

a month for survival strategies

JOB FILE

- *Mulch, mulch, mulch!*
- *Water plants deeply during dry periods*
- *Inspect potted plants daily for moisture content*
- *Raise mower blades high before cutting lawns in southern states, but keep them low in the north*
- *Clean up garden rubbish near houses in bushfire areas*
- *Plant flower and vegetable seedlings from September and October container sowings, but keep them moist*

The Australian summer can be hard on gardens, and December is a good month for ensuring their survival. You will find that there is quite a lot you can do to temper the heat, although at least a few days each year will test your plants and your patience to their limits – and perhaps well beyond that point.

choose the right plants for your climate

Plants that look good in December but are scorched by the end of February are sometimes flourishing again a few months later. These are well worth keeping. But if too many of your plants actually die in summer, you probably need to replace them with tougher species.

Many Australian natives resist dryness as well as heat. There are also plenty of exotics that withstand dryness, including the hardy succulents that were mentioned in November as drought-resisters (see 'Small plants for dry spots', page 173). Always check a plant's moisture needs before you buy it.

water appropriately

In southern states, where the summer is normally fairly dry, a certain amount of artificial watering is essential. Be sure to follow the water-usage laws in your area.

Coastal gardens from Sydney northwards have a different pattern. Summer temperatures are high, but most of the year's rain falls between November and April; in some districts artificial watering may be needed only occasionally at this time of year.

Wherever you live, the following kinds of plants need watching, with daily watering in hot, dry weather:

- vegetables
- annual flowers
- trees, shrubs and climbers that were planted in spring
- plants in pots and hanging baskets.

Autumn and early-winter planting of ornamentals is often suggested as a way of establishing them thoroughly before summer.

In southern states this should reduce their need for supplementary watering; in the north it should allow them to make good growth before being bombarded by summer storms and downpours.

Some gardeners turn on a hose only when they see plants drooping. There are certainly plants that can cope with such treatment; others – especially shallow-rooted species and newly planted ones – are likely to succumb if they are not watered before they begin to wilt.

water effectively

No matter where you live, water is a precious commodity so use it as efficiently as possible.

- Water early in the morning or during the evening to minimise evaporation.
- Water for long enough to allow moisture to penetrate below root level.
- Install tap-timers to turn the water on and off for you.
- Investigate an automatic dripper or sprinkler system.
- Water indoor and outdoor container plants deep down by dunking occasionally in a bucket or trough of water (remove containers when bubbles stop rising).

mulch thoroughly

Mulching will help your garden survive the summer. It puts a kind of thermal blanket over the roots of plants, keeping them cool and reducing evaporation from the surface of the soil. Mulching also suppresses the growth of weeds, which compete with plants for moisture. All mulches should be spread 5–15 cm thick, but need to be kept back 3–4 cm from the stems or trunks of plants. Water garden beds thoroughly before and after mulching.

Mulches may be inorganic or organic. Inorganic mulches, such as gravel or coarse sand, are effective coolers, but they do not add value to the soil. Organic mulches, such as lawn clippings, rot down and provide beneficial humus. To offset the nitrogen taken up by organic mulches as they decompose, a couple of matchboxfuls of sulphate of ammonia should be dissolved in water for sprinkling around (*not* over) plants about once a year, or whenever you notice that leaves are yellowing.

The following are all organic mulches:

- wood shavings and wood chips
- sawdust
- pine bark
- shredded garden refuse
- home-made compost

- weeds (preferably with no seedheads)
- twigs and leaves
- straw (almost weedless)
- hay (likely to produce many weeds, easily pulled)
- lawn clippings (preferably dried for a day or two first)
- seaweed
- animal manure.

One of the best organic mulches is mushroom compost, the rich, weed-free, slightly alkaline material specially prepared for commercial mushroom-growing and discarded after use.

Other local industries may have waste products that make good mulch. The possibilities include:

- grape marc (from wineries)
- cottonseed by-products (from cotton mills)
- macadamia and other nut shells
- bagasse (cane residue from sugar mills – all used up for boiler fuel in some mills, but worth inquiring about)
- spent hops (from breweries).

protect yourself too
- Wear a hat and keep your arms and legs covered.
- Cover exposed skin with sunscreen.

- Avoid working in the garden, if possible, between 11 a.m. and 3 p.m. in summer.

cool & temperate zones

December is a month for reducing fire danger by removing garden debris and other rubbish from near the house and composting it, or incinerating it before fire bans are posted. Gutters and downpipes may need leaves and twiggery removed, and branches should be cut back if they are too close to buildings.

flowers to plant

Seed	*Seedlings*
aster	ageratum
cosmos	alyssum
Iceland poppy*	aster
lupin	carnation
nasturtium*	cosmos

COOL & TEMPERATE ZONES

flowers . . . seed

pansy
petunia
phlox*
portulaca
Virginian stock*
viscaria*
zinnia

vegetables to plant

Seed

bean, French*
beetroot*
broccoli
cabbage
capsicum
carrot*
cauliflower
cucumber*
lettuce*
marrow*

flowers . . . seedlings

lupin
petunia
portulaca
salvia
verbena
zinnia

Seedlings

broccoli
cabbage
capsicum
cauliflower
celery
eggplant
leek
silver beet
spinach
tomato

vegetables . . . seed
melon*
onion, white*
parsnip*
pea*
pumpkin*
radish*
silver beet
spinach
sweetcorn*
zucchini*

*Seed of these plants is best sown straight into the garden. Others should be sown in containers for transplanting later, or may be available now as seedlings.

other jobs for december

- Pot up cuttings of house-plants and shrubs as Christmas presents.
- Water the garden section by section to cover it all regularly. Use a soil-wetting agent if water tends to run off.
- Buy some summer seedlings to fill gaps in flower beds.
- Make traps for earwigs from matchboxes or small tins (laid on their side) partly filled with straw or shredded paper. Destroy the insects each morning.

COOL & TEMPERATE ZONES

- Pick strawberries daily.
- Prune side shoots of tomatoes, and stake tall varieties.
- Hand-pollinate flowering pumpkins if fruit is not setting: dust pollen from male flowers (smaller) into the centre of female flowers.
- Thin out beetroot, carrot, lettuce and parsnip seedlings.
- Prepare house plants for a stay on their own when you are going on holiday. Put a plastic garbage bag in the bath, lay a whole newspaper on it, and put the well-watered pots on the paper. Run the tap until the paper is saturated, then pull out the plug.
- Plant dahlia tubers and gladiolus corms.
- Take softwood and semi-hardwood cuttings.
- Look for pear and cherry slug on leaves of hawthorns, plums, pears, cherries and quinces. Talcum powder works well on small areas; or spray with pyrethrum or carbaryl.
- Spray apple and pear trees every three weeks with carbaryl against codling moth and light brown apple moth.
- Lift ranunculus and anemones. Cut off dead flowerheads and hang stems (with swollen roots attached) to dry under cover.
- Deadhead roses.
- Trim climbers such as jasmine, honeysuckle, wisteria and hardenbergia if they are spreading too far.

- Sprinkle fuchsias with liquid fertiliser.
- Erect sun shelters, if necessary, to protect plants like hydrangeas.

fire-resistant plants

The following plants have a reputation as fire-retarders. If you live in an area prone to bushfire, be sure to include some of them in your planting.

Trees:

- *Angophora costata* (smooth-barked apple)
- *Calodendrum capense* (Cape chestnut)
- *Eucalyptus maculata* (spotted gum)
- *Pittosporum undulatum* (sweet pittosporum)

Shrubs:

- *Camellia* species and cultivars
- *Hakea salicifolia* (willow-leaved hakea)
- *Hydrangea* species
- *Photinia glabra* (redleaf photinia)

Small plants:

- *Atriplex nummularia* (old man saltbush, and other saltbushes)
- *Dichondra repens* : (kidneyweed)
- *Myoporum parvifolium* (creeping boobialla)

looking good down south

- Noble spikes of grey and white acanthus; pink and white butterfly flowers on gaura; tall foxgloves and delphiniums; brilliant-red Jacobean lily
- Fuchsias in garden beds and hanging baskets; roses and lavender at their best
- Cape chestnut (*Calodendrum capense*), covered with arresting clusters of spidery pink flowers

subtropical & tropical zones

Downpours and gale-force winds can damage northern gardens in summer. Cyclones occasionally devastate them.

Fungal diseases sometimes become evident, fostered by the high humidity, and spraying with a fungicide may be necessary.

Mulching is particularly important at this time of year.

flowers to plant

Seed	*Seedlings*
ageratum	ageratum
celosia	celosia
coleus	coleus
salvia	cosmos
torenia	salvia
	torenia
	zinnia

vegetables to plant

Seed	*Seedlings*
capsicum	cabbage
cucumber*	capsicum
eggplant	eggplant
lettuce*	silver beet
marrow*	
melon*	
pumpkin*	
radish*	
silver beet	

SUBTROPICAL & TROPICAL ZONES

SUBTROPICAL & TROPICAL ZONES

vegetables . . . seed
sweetcorn*
zucchini*

*Seed of these plants is best sown straight into the garden. Others should be sown in containers for transplanting later, or may be available now as seedlings.

other jobs for december

- Pot up cuttings of house-plants and shrubs as Christmas presents.
- Prune the orange browallia (*Streptosolen jamesonii*) to keep the shrub compact.
- Plant new lawns.
- Maintain fruit fly baits in fruit trees and continue to spray with fenthion. Destroy fallen fruit.
- Make traps for earwigs from matchboxes or small tins (laid on their side) partly filled with straw or shredded paper. Destroy the insects each morning.
- Try layering an azalea by making a small cut under a low branch and pinning it to the ground under 5 cm of soil. When layered stem is well rooted and growing, separate it from the shrub and then plant it.
- Take softwood and semi-hardwood cuttings to grow new plants.

- Prune poinsettia again early this month.
- Plant sweet potatoes in the vegetable garden.
- Prune and stake shallow-rooted shrubs to protect them against strong winds.
- Look out for lawn armyworms (dark brown caterpillars, with bodies wider than their heads). Spray with dipel (a safe biological spray) or carbaryl.
- Plant tropical fruit trees.

looking good up north

- The white flowers of the Christmas orchid (*Calanthe triplicata*) arising from large, shiny leaves
- Silky oak (*Grevillea robusta*), with enormous orange brush flowers
- Two trees that look stunning together are poinciana (*Delonix regia*), with red flowers, and jacaranda (*Jacaranda mimosifolia*), with mauve flowers

cool-looking corners

A soothing patch of ferns – a damp, green corner – can make your garden seem cooler in the hot weather. The soil should be well drained but must be kept fairly moist: an automatic system simplifies the watering. Shade, or dappled shade, is necessary, and so is

SUBTROPICAL & TROPICAL ZONES

protection from wind. Mulch your ferns with leaf mould or peat moss if possible.

Include some Australian species in your fern garden. Here are some varieties to try:

Medium to tall:

- *Adiantum formosum* (black stem maidenhair)
- *Blechnum nudum* (fishbone water fern)
- *Cyathea cooperi* (tree fern)

Small:

- *Adiantum aethiopicum* (maidenhair fern)
- *Blechnum patersonii* (strap water fern)
- *Doodia caudata* (small rasp fern)

Conditions suitable for ferns encourage the natural growth of velvety mosses. A ferny corner can be established in a garden anywhere in Australia provided that moisture and shade are available.

index